THE EAST COAST
BED &
BREAKFAST
GUIDE

Front entrance to Isaac Stover House, Erwinna, Pennsylvania.

NEW ENGLAND AND THE MID-ATLANTIC

Bed & Breakfast Guide
EAST COAST

BY ROBERTA GARDNER, NAOMI BLACK,
TERRY BERGER, ROBERT REID, AND GALE ZUCKER

Photographs by George W. Gardner,
and Gale Zucker

DESIGNED AND PRODUCED BY
ROBERT R. REID AND TERRY BERGER

PRENTICE HALL TRAVEL

NEW YORK   LONDON   TORONTO   SYDNEY   TOKYO   SINGAPORE

A Robert Reid / Terry Berger production
Typeset in Bodoni Book by Monotype Composition Company,
Baltimore
Produced by Mandarin Offset, Hong Kong
Printed in Hong Kong

1 2 3 4 5 6 7 8 9 10

Library of Congress Cataloging-in-Publication Data

Bed & breakfast guide : East Coast / [edited by] Gale Zucker
. . . [et al.].
    p. cm.
    Includes index.
    ISBN 0-13-068420-1 : $15.00
    1. Bed and breakfast accommodations—New England—
Guide-books.
    2. Bed and breakfast accommodations—Middle Atlantic
States—Guidebooks. I. Zucker, Gale. II. Title: Bed and
breakfast guide.
TX907.3.N35B43   1991
647.947403—dc20   91-2108
                                 CIP

CONTENTS

continued overleaf

PENNSYLVANIA

NEW JERSEY

MARYLAND

WASHINGTON, D.C.

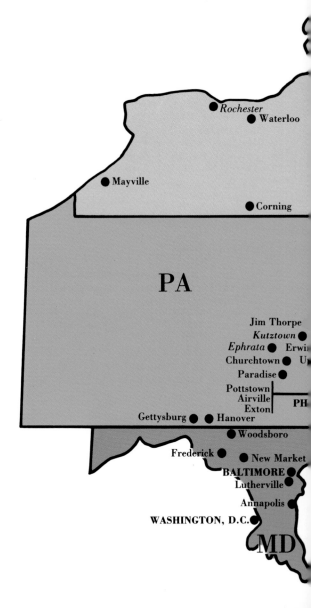

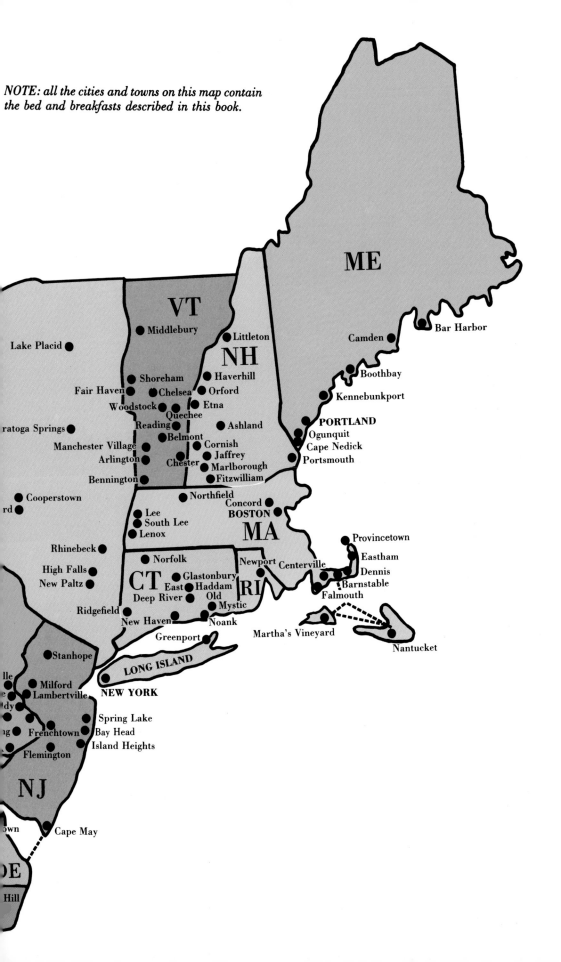

NOTE: all the cities and towns on this map contain
the bed and breakfasts described in this book.

ME

VT

Middlebury • • Littleton

Lake Placid • NH

Camden • • Bar Harbor

Shoreham • • Haverhill Boothbay •

Fair Haven • • Chelsea • Orford Kennebunkport

Woodstock • • Etna

Quechee

ratoga Springs • Reading • • Ashland PORTLAND •

Belmont • Ogunquit

Manchester Village • Cornish Cape Nedick

Arlington • Chester • Jaffrey Portsmouth •

Bennington • Marlborough

• Fitzwilliam

Cooperstown • • Northfield

rd • Concord •

Lee • BOSTON •

South Lee • MA

Lenox • Provincetown •

Rhinebeck • Norfolk • Eastham

High Falls • Newport • Centerville Dennis

New Paltz • CT Glastonbury Barnstable

East Haddam RI Falmouth

Deep River Old

Ridgefield • Mystic

New Haven • Noank Martha's Vineyard

Greenport • Nantucket •

Stanhope • LONG ISLAND

lle • Milford NEW YORK

e • Lambertville

dy •

Spring Lake

ng • Frenchtown • Bay Head

Flemington Island Heights

NJ

wn • Cape May

DE

Hill

MAINE

Artful Lodgings

The soft-grey façade of this Victorian reveals nothing of its interior. But, open the door and surprises burst forth as they do from a Fabergé Easter egg. A real treat is in store for you!

Isabel and Alan Smiles, collectors of museum-quality art, and decorators *extraordinaire*, have produced a house that is difficult to leave. Heidi Gerquest's hand-painted designs on bedroom walls— from fantasy birds to roses in bloom—would inspire Matisse. American, English, and Chinese antiques blend harmoniously with Oriental floor coverings and hand-painted floors. Hand-lacquered halls feature modern-crafted pieces that enliven the space. Bathrooms with Grecian-marbled floors and faux-marbled touches on cornices and tubs are not to be missed.

Left, two of the superb guest rooms, showing the decorative walls that were painted by hand.

CHUCK NEAVES PHOTOGRAPH

Our color coordinated author, Terry Berger, blends perfectly with the handpainted walls of a Pomegranate guest room.

You keep wishing you could sleep in *all* the guest rooms. A Johnny Ross painting, Jamie Burt's perfect egg, and Tommy Simpson's whimsical cupboard vie for attention. And covering the walls are the vibrant watercolors and sensual floral oil paintings by artist Winifred Mury, the Smiles' relative who painted for over 60 years, and predicted that she would be famous only after she died.

A hot breakfast prepared by the host is served on a hand-painted table, and is so artfully presented that it becomes a part of the surrounding art collection.

Staying here offers you the pleasure of meeting wonderful people who appreciate and collect beautiful things, and are willing to share their treasures with their guests.

THE POMEGRANATE INN, 49 Neal Street, Portland, ME 04102; (207) 772-1006; (800) 356-0408; Fax (207) 773-4426; Alan and Isabel Smiles, owners. Open all year. Six guest rooms with private baths. Rates: $95 per room ($10 less off season), including full breakfast. Children over 16 welcome; no pets; smoking in public rooms only; Visa/MasterCard. Portland's charmingly restored historic district is alive with restaurants and shops. The Portland Museum of Art is also highly recommended.

DIRECTIONS: call for directions, which vary depending on where you are.

CLEFTSTONE MANOR

Preserves the mood of Victorian gentility

James Blair built his summer home, a modest thirty-three room cottage, high on a rocky ledge overlooking the beautiful isle of Bar Harbor. His winter home in Washington, D.C., later used as an alternate presidential residence known as Blair House, sat across from the White House. Today both homes welcome travelers, Blair House serving as a home to dignitaries visiting the United States. Cleftstone Manor, under the thoughtful ownership of Phyllis and Donald Jackson, is a supremely lovely bed and breakfast inn.

The entire house is furnished with fine antiques, including such unusual pieces as Joseph Pulitzer's awesome writing table. This grand table amply fills the formal dining room and is put to use each day when it is laden with scones and shortbread at tea time and with cheeses and wine in the evening. Breakfast is served on the enclosed sunporch, a light-washed room complemented by white wicker furniture, a collection of Delft china, and masses of greenery.

The bedrooms, each different, are decorated with a confident and sophisticated touch. A favorite for honeymooners is the spacious Romeo and Juliet Room. One corner is given over to a brass canopied bed, draped in white lace. A comfortable love seat faces a working fireplace and the beautifully detailed coffered ceiling deepens the prevailing sense of privacy and luxury. The Glastonbury Room, with high-back Victorian bedstead, red velvet chair, hand-crocheted bedspread, and many decorative grace notes is serene.

CLEFTSTONE MANOR, Eden St., Bar Harbor, ME 04609; (207) 288-4951; Phyllis and Donald Jackson and family, hosts. Open May 15 to Oct. 15. Thirteen double rooms, three suites, four with fireplaces, three with balconies; mostly private baths. Rates: $75 double, shared baths, $85 to $150, private baths; rates include breakfast buffet with emphasis on home baking. Evening wine and cheese. Numerous restaurants nearby. Children over 12 welcome; no pets; Visa/MasterCard/American Express. The Jacksons are also proprietors of the nearby Tides Mansion, an ocean front estate.

DIRECTIONS: from points south, take Rte. 1 north to Ellsworth, then follow Rte. 3 into Bar Harbor. Inn is 500 feet past Bluenose Ferry terminal.

Joseph Pulitzer's writing table in the formal dining room.

A stunning brass bed in an airy guest room.

The original wood-paneled reception hall.

NORUMBEGA

An extraordinary stone mansion

Norumbega is an extraordinary stone mansion whose elusive exterior seems to change when viewed at different angles. Designed by A.B. Jennings of New York City, the Queen Anne style manse is quite unique. From one angle the house shows a wall of roughly faced cobblestones, punctuated by arched windows and a rounded, stepped roof. From another, it resembles a more common seaside cottage with a wide porch and bay windows. Looking at the entrance, the *porte cocherè*, and turret, the structure appears to be predominantly wood and brick. Close inspection reveals at least three different shingle patterns on the turret, the name "Norumbega" and "1886"

tiled and set in the right bay, and fossils embedded in the stone to the left of the entrance.

Inside, the wood draws first notice. Triangular-sawn oak with a marked sheen forms the entryway and three stairs to a landing with fireplace and elaborately carved corner seating. Spiral spindles below the banister add a suitably delicate touch.

The double parlors and curved study boast their share of beautiful wood. Carved grotesques, as compelling as Notre Dame's gargoyles, flank the fireplace; a central wood carpet establishes the floor theme.

The house, now restored to its full elegance, is a stunning home complete with mountain and water views. Murray and Elisabeth Keatinge, the owners, afford gracious service and warm hospitality.

NORUMBEGA, 61 High St., Camden, ME 04843; (207) 236-4646; Murray and Elisabeth Keatinge, hosts. Open all year. Twelve guest rooms, all with private baths, five with working fireplaces. Rates: $135 to $195; additional person, $50; includes generous, full breakfast. Children over 7 welcome; no pets; smoking permitted; all credit cards. Hiking, skiing, tennis, golf, ocean beach and freshwater lake, windjammer cruises, Lighthouse Museum in Rockland. Good restaurants.

DIRECTIONS: follow Rte. 1 north through Camden. The inn is on the right about one mile from town.

A 1786 colonial building.

KENNISTON HILL INN

Once a country club

History helps make the inn a special place. Three separate entrances from its days as an apartment house add a welcome bit of privacy. Still, guests often choose to gather in front of the living room fireplace. The two-hundred-year-old cherry mantelpiece forms a nesting place for wooden ducks and assorted baskets. A collection of handmade and acquired stained glass light-catchers decorate the paned window wall.

Paul and Ellen Morisette retired to Kenniston Hill, giving up their Country Kitchen restaurant in Brattleboro, Vermont. "It's never humid here like Vermont. We don't need air conditioning. The windows are always open for breezes," Ellen says happily, "and now we have time to talk to people." They also have time to prepare an outstanding breakfast of such fare as delicately sauced eggs Benedict, fresh asparagus, and fluffy light popovers. Artfully presented fresh fruit pleases the eye as well as the palate.

KENNISTON HILL INN, Rte. 27, Boothbay, ME 04537; (207) 633-2159; Paul and Ellen Morissette, hosts. Open April through November. White clapboard colonial built in 1786, on 4½ acres. Eight guest rooms, four with working fireplaces, all with private baths. Rates: $60 to $80, double; $10 for additional person. Full breakfast served. Children over ten preferred; no pets; MasterCard/Visa. Bicycles available at no charge; 9-hole golf nearby. Varied dining at the harbor.

DIRECTIONS: from Rte. 1 turn onto Rte. 27 south to Boothbay. The inn is on a knoll on the left.

The breakfast room, like most of the house, is furnished simply in deference to the colonial tradition. Pale yellow pineapple paper picks up the soft specks of gold and brown in the braided rug and the tawny hues of the pine sideboard. What makes Kenniston Hill most appealing, though, are the four guest rooms with working fireplaces. A spotlessly maintained colonial restoration, Kenniston Hill is perfect for all-season beachcombers and high-season sailors.

Beamed ceilings and a 200-year-old cherry mantel.

FIVE GABLES INN

Quiet serenity

The Five Gables Inn is ideally situated for travelers who want to get away from other tourists. It is a haven of peace and quiet overlooking the water at the end of a winding country road, where the only sounds to be heard are the cries of seagulls wheeling overhead.

Local innkeepers Ellen and Paul Morissette recognized the potential of the unused inn. It had been a haven to the former owners when they arrived in the 1930s, as refugees from Nazi Germany.

Protected as a landmark, the inn was restored and rebuilt at the same time. Today, it offers all the latest amenities along with the flavor of painted wooden V-joint carpentry.

The walls of the rooms and hallways have been tastefully decorated by the Morissette's daughter-in-law, Nadine, with a variety of serigraphs, lithographs, old photographs, dried flowers, crazy quilts, and even framed needlepoint pictures.

One welcome addition to the original design is a large veranda that overlooks the water, as does the large public reception room, where a full breakfast is served buffet-style. Paul was a restaurateur for twenty years, and has developed a menu that varies from quiches and chili stratas to blueberry pancakes, French toast with maple syrup, and egg dishes with homemade biscuits—all served with fresh fruit.

FIVE GABLES INN, Murray Hill Rd., East Boothbay, ME 04544; (207) 633-4551; Ellen and Paul Morissette, owners. Open mid-May to mid-Nov. Fourteen guest rooms with private baths; 5 with working fireplaces, all with views, except one. Rates: $80 to $120 per room, including full buffet breakfast. Children over 12 welcome; no pets; smoking on verandah only; Visa/MasterCard. Excellent seafood restaurants, including Maxfield's and Russell House in Boothbay Harbor. Theater, excursion boats, lighthouses, old forts.

DIRECTIONS: from Portland take I-95 north to exit 22 to Brunswick and U.S. 1 east to Rte. 27 south towards Boothbay Harbor. At junction with Rte. 96 turn left on 96 and wind past shipyard to general store and junction with Murrary Hill Rd., which should be followed to inn at end of road.

Even on a cloudy day, the view at breakfast time is exhiliarting.

Elegant four-poster beds in beautifully decorated guest rooms.

THE TIDES

Rooms with a view

The Tides, one of Bar Harbor's beautiful old summer cottages, is an 1887 white-columned Greek Revival with an acre of lawn stretching down to the ocean. Located on Frenchman's Bay in the historic part of town, the eighteen-room home is elegantly proportioned. There is a wrap-around porch with working fireplace that guests adore, and the white wicker furniture allows them to sit and enjoy the fire, the ocean, and the bountiful breakfast that is usually served there—perhaps a spinach quiche, a vegetable

strata, or stuffed French toast.

Three light and airy rooms are available for guests, including the master suite with a working fireplace. All of the rooms are turned out in Laura Ashley finery, and all offer full ocean views.

The formal dining room has cherrywood furniture and a fireplace, and the most amazing twenty-one foot window seat and picture windows overlooking the Atlantic. The parlor, bathed in pastel greens and mauve, is adorned with an 1868 Chickering piano, three overstuffed sofas, and of course, a water view.

Sunset schooner sailing, sea kayaking, and nature cruises are popular activities. The bed and breakfast is one block from the town pier and within walking distance of town, where there are fine restaurants and gift shops.

Majestically beautiful Acadia National Park, a legacy of the Rockefellers, occupies most of the island. It offers countless trails for hiking, horseback riding, bicycling, and cross-country skiing.

THE TIDES, 119 West Street, Bar Harbor, ME 04609; (207) 288-4968; Katy and Jed Wood, innkeepers. Open May 1 to Nov. 1. Three guest rooms with private baths, queen-sized beds, and ocean views. Rates: $150 to $175 high season; $130 to $150 off season. Includes full breakfast. Children over 12 welcome; no pets; no smoking; Visa/MasterCard.

DIRECTIONS: take Rte. 3 into Bar Harbor and turn left on West St. at first intersection (no light, but there is an island).

INN AT HARBOR HEAD

Right on Maine's lobster coast

Artistry, elegance, and natural beauty in equal measure are the prime qualities of life at the Inn at Harbor Head. This intimate bed and breakfast is located on Kennebunkport's Cape Porpoise Bay, an idyllic lobstering cove whose sparkling waters are dotted with bobbing boats, rocky islands, and lighthouses that twinkle in the distance. Joan and Dave Sutter own the inn, a turn-of-the-century, weathered-shingle home that rambles along a promontory overlooking a sheltered harbor and the bay beyond.

Inside, the Sutters have created an elegant world that is sophisticated enough for the pages of a stylish home magazine. The inn's common rooms are furnished in a refined style, the living room displaying a crystal chandelier, a handsome Japanese screen, fine oriental rugs, and softly-lit oil paintings of the Sutters' ancestors. But real artistry is revealed in the five guest bedrooms. Joan is a seasoned artist—or, in her words, "a former three-dimensional artist now changed to 'wall painter' "—whose genius for color and de-

sign is wedded to an equally accomplished technical skill. Each bedroom plays out a romantic theme embellished by Joan's lyrical, painted imaginings inspired by the bay and surrounding village. The walls and ceiling of the Harbor Suite, for example, are decorated with soft and expressive murals that picture sailboats gliding across azure water; white herons stalking food in a shallow marsh; billowing white clouds on a field of soft blue; and a mother bird feeding eager fledglings.

The Sutters pamper their guests at breakfasttime, serving fresh-squeezed orange juice and fresh fruits, savory entrées, and fresh-baked breads. All may be savored amid the cut crystal and antique pewter in the dining room, or on the patio overlooking the water.

THE INN AT HARBOR HEAD, Pier Road, Cape Porpoise, RR 2, Box 1180, Kennebunkport, ME 04046; (207) 967-5564; Dave and Joan Sutter, hosts. Open all year, except for 2 weeks in the spring and Nov. Five rooms with private baths. Rates: $95 to $175, with full gourmet breakfast. Children over 12 welcome; no pets; Visa/MasterCard; smoke-free environment; a little Japanese spoken. Swimming from inn's dock. Whale watching, art galleries, summer theater, antiquing in area. Dining nearby.

DIRECTIONS: from Maine Turnpike take exit 3 and follow Rte. 9 east through Kennebunkport Village to Cape Porpoise. Leave Rte. 9 at hardware store and take the road to the pier for ³⁄₁₀ miles to inn on right.

The Harbor Suite has hand-painted murals in both rooms.

Breakfast room in the main house.

OLD FORT INN

Kennebunkport charm

The Old Fort Inn is a charming carriage house-lodge combination that invites travelers for long-term stays. The sixteen color-coordinated American and English country-style rooms come with cable color television, some with efficiency kitchens stocked with ironstone plates, wine glasses, pans, tea kettle, toaster, napkins and placemats—even laundry facilities.

It's one-and-a-fifth miles from the inn to town, an easy bike ride past lovely frame cottages and old sea captains' houses. Kennebunkport retains much of its late nineteenth-century atmosphere when ship building gave way to the tourist industry. Wealthy summer visitors built wisely and well, keeping the village quaint and relatively small. The inn's location, just one block from the rocky shore, is also adjacent to Cape Arundel, where some of the most handsome turn-of-the-century cottages still stand.

Kennebunkport offers a rich variety of activities: trolley rides, scenic cruises, sailing lessons, yacht charters, and whale watching are but a few. The sports menu complements what the Old Fort Inn has to offer on its grounds. A swimming pool, shuffleboard area, and tennis court bridge the gap between the guest rooms and the main lodge where breakfast is served.

Sheila and David Aldrich and their daughter oversee the homemade muffins, fresh-baked breads, and fresh fruit for the buffet breakfast. Friendships often begin at the morning meal and extend into the evening hours around the pool.

The Old Fort Inn presents the best of what casual adult resorts can provide: a relaxed atmosphere amid pleasant surroundings.

OLD FORT INN, Old Fort Ave., Kennebunkport, ME 04046; (207) 967-5353; Sheila and David Aldrich, hosts. Open April 26 to mid-December. Fourteen guest rooms plus two suites, all with private baths and efficiency kitchens or wet bars; some with Jacuzzis. Rates: $98 to $155; suites, $175 to $210; additional person, $15. Rates include buffet breakfast and one hour of tennis daily. Children over 12 welcome; no pets; no cigars and pipes in bedrooms; pool on premises. American Express/MasterCard/Visa/Discover.

DIRECTIONS: take exit 3 from I-95 and turn left on Rte. 35 for 5½ miles. Turn left at light at Sunoco station and go .3 miles to Colony Hotel and turn left and follow signs to inn.

Each guest room has a kitchenette.

A spacious third-floor guest room

CAPTAIN JEFFERDS INN

A New England sea captain's house

The Kennebunkport historic district is peppered with gracious "cottages" built in the early 1800s by seafaring captains who traveled the globe in pursuit of treasure.

Warren Fitzsimmons and Don Kelly were partners in a successful antiques business when they bought one of these—Captain Jefferds' home—and brought the place to vibrant life. If, upon entering, you have a sense of déjà vu, don't doubt your feelings. The work of these two gifted innkeepers has been featured on the covers of several prestigious home decorating magazines. Two cobalt blue vases displaying a bounty of brilliant silk flowers flank the formal entryway. To the left is the breakfast room where guests gather each morning to be served by Don, dressed in butler's whites. Warren mans the kitchen, serving up custardy French toast, delicate pancakes, and perfectly turned eggs.

Each bedroom is special. Several are decorated in Laura Ashley's simple prints; others are dressed in muted tones that dramatize an elegant chaise, bird's-eye maple chest, or Chinese screen.

The collection of antiques in this inn is endlessly fascinating. Warren and Don buy only the truest examples of a representative period—there are no reproductions in the entire inn—and the place practically vibrates from the beauty produced by their combined collections. Though Warren and Don were personally attracted to American antiques, from tramp and shell art to twig furniture and Indian baskets, the inn's formal lines required sterling silver and crystal as well. It all works.

THE CAPTAIN JEFFERDS INN , Pearl St., P.O. Box 691, Kennebunkport, ME 04046; (207) 967-2311; Warren Fitzsimmons, host. 1804 Federal style sea captain's house. Open all year except closed during January, February, March. Twelve guest rooms in main house, all private baths; three efficiency apartments in carriage house. Rates $85 single, $85 to $125 double; apartments $125–135 per day, in season; guests in main house are treated to full breakfast, with seasonal specialties. No children under twelve; pets welcome, with advance notice; smoking not permitted in dining room; no credit cards.

DIRECTIONS: take Maine Turnpike to exit 3 to Rte. 35. Follow signs through Kennebunk to Kennebunkport. Turn left at traffic light and cross drawbridge. Turn right at monument onto Ocean Ave. Proceed ³⁄₁₀ mile to Arundel Wharf and turn left onto Pearl St.

WOODEN GOOSE INN

A stunning restoration

Right off Route 1, sometimes called the "antique row of New England," the Wooden Goose Inn corners off its own country garden in full view of the Cape Neddick River. Guests gazing out from the glassed-in breakfast room overlook the perennial blooms and a specially commissioned Chippendale garden bench. The bench is just one of interior designer Jerry Rippetoe's unique additions to this intimate country house. Partner Tony Sienicki, the other half of this able team, attends to most of the carpentry and finishing.

The precision restoration began June 15, 1983, the day they bought the house. By July 2, after working twenty-two-hour days, Jerry and Tony welcomed their first overnight visitors. The quick revitalization succeeded only because of professional foresight and months of planning and preparation. "The day we looked at it we took measurements," remarked Tony.

The result is stunning. A true overabundance of Victorian paraphernalia blends with revitalized Orientalia. The focus in the reception room rests

on the hand-carved, hand-painted cormondel screen, a black lacquer on teak *chef-d'oeuvre* that hints at other treasures inside. Guests are rarely disappointed with the many beautiful touches.

Excess and elegance are synonymous here. Twenty-eight yards of chintz drape down from one canopy. The clawfoot tub of bedroom number 4 stands in regal spaciousness next to a bentwood rocker, a combination that inspires guests to bring their own bubble bath and champagne.

Morning starts with elaborate breakfasts served on Lenox china with silver and linen asides. Plans to replace Sheelan crystal with Waterford illustrate the dynamics of the Wooden Goose. Every January the doors close for redecoration. Balloon shades change to miniblinds; greens give way to blues. The transformation keeps the inn vital—and keeps guests returning year after year.

THE WOODEN GOOSE INN , Rte. 1, Cape Neddick, ME 03902; (207) 363-5673; Tony Sienicki and Jerry Rippetoe, hosts. Open February through December. Six guest rooms, all with private baths. Rates: $95 to $105; suite, $150; including an elegant, hearty breakfast which changes every day. Afternoon tea. Dining nearby. Children over 12 welcome; no pets; no credit cards. The ocean is one mile from the inn. Golf, tennis, and bicycling in Ogunquit.

DIRECTIONS: take I-95 to the York exit (No. 1, marked "last exit before toll"). Turn north on Rte. 1 for 3.4 miles. The inn is on the right, five houses after the junction of Rtes. 1 and 1A.

The sunny lounge and breakfast room.

HARTWELL HOUSE

Lifestyles of the rich and famous

The Hartwell House is as close to perfect as life allows. When things seem out of control, this is a special oasis that offers solace, serenity, and service. Every need is anticipated by innkeepers Trisha and Jim Hartwell to insure that all is flawless for the duration of your stay.

Furnished with period pieces of simple elegance in the main house, and a more contemporary and lighter feeling in the House on the Hill across the way, the feeling is similar in both—a successful blending of the outdoors with the interior space, in colors so pure and furnishings so simple that it has a calming effect on guests.

Balconies with picture-perfect flower boxes look over Perkins Cove, once a famous artists' colony, and now a bustling sea village of lobster shacks, restaurants, boutiques, and shops. All of this is just a mile from the sand dunes and the beautiful three-mile beach.

The Abenaki Indians' word Ogunquit means "Beautiful Place by the Sea." The same can be said about the Hartwell House.

HARTWELL HOUSE, 118 Shore Road, Ogunquit, ME 03907; (207) 646-7210; Jim and Trisha Hartwell, Ted and Judith Kolva, innkeepers. Open all year. Sixteen rooms and suites in 2 houses, all with private baths and parking. Rates: $100 to $175 double, including continental buffet breakfast (off-season rates after Nov. 1, including full breakfast). Inquire about children, as there are no special facilities; no pets; no smoking; Visa/MasterCard/American Express. Extravagant seafood dining within walking distance at famous Perkins Cove, just down the road. Beaches and dunes for fresh air and swimming. Golf privileges at Cape Neddick Country Club.

DIRECTIONS: from Portland take scenic Rte. 1 through Ogunquit/Shore Road to inn.

The décor is elegantly restrained.

NEW HAMPSHIRE

SISE INN

Restored to its former glory

Home to one of the area's leading maritime merchants when Portsmouth was "the fishing and ship-building capital of the New World," the Sise Inn has been restored to its former glory.

Owned by a group that restores historic properties as bed and breakfasts in the United States and Canada, the Sise Inn provides comforts and amenities that suit the business traveler and tourist alike. Twenty-five rooms and nine suites individually decorated in period pieces, easily accommodate families and groups. Original carved woodwork, moldings, and decorative fireplaces supply interest and warmth.

Left, top, the inviting breakfast room; bottom, guest rooms offer a variety of décors.

Served in the breakfast room every morning, a buffet includes muffins, bagels, yogurt, cheese, and cereals. Breakfast may also be enjoyed on the adjoining sun porch.

Restaurants in the area that merit mention are The Dolphin Striker, as well as The Library Restaurant, which is located in the old Rockingham mansion which dates back to 1785. The Library Restaurant features American cuisine, and shelves filled with yards of vintage books.

Sise Inn managers Gisele and Carl Jensen are eager to please, and Carl is the recipient of the New Hampshire Innkeeping Award for 1989. Guests will most certainly find an award-winning bed and breakfast here.

SISE INN, 40 Court Street, Portsmouth, NH 03801; (603) 433-1200; Carl and Gisele Jensen, managers. Open all year. 34 guest rooms, all with private baths. Rates: $89 to $150 double, including continental breakfast buffet. Children welcome; no pets; smoking allowed; Danish spoken; Visa/MasterCard/American Express/Diners Club. Inn has 3 conference and reception rooms with audio-visual equipment.

DIRECTIONS: right off I-95 in downtown Portsmouth; ask for detailed directions.

LEIGHTON INN

Colonial elegance

The elegance and refinement of the colonial period is showcased in the Leighton Inn, located within an easy walk of Portsmouth's historic Old Harbor. The house, a classic white clapboard finished with Federal detailing, was built in 1809 and thoroughly refurbished in the 1980s. Innkeeper Catherine Stone fell in love with the building's clean, strong lines, which she instantly knew would harmonize with her collection of antique Empire furnishings. In combining the two, Catherine created a serene and inviting bed and breakfast inn, a peaceful haven filled with books, music, and flowers.

Furnishings and window treatments throughout the inn are in keeping with the Federal period. Catherine researched authentic Federal colors as well, and chose from that palette deep rose, butter yellow, rich blue, and mustard gold to accent rooms. She then furnished each simple and pristine bedroom with antiques from her extensive collection.

Each morning Catherine treats guests to a generous and leisurely breakfast which, in summer, is savored on the screened-in porch, the better to enjoy the inn's fragrant perennials garden. Breakfast is hearty, and it includes juice and fresh fruit (including home-grown raspberries, in season); cinnamon-blueberry or Scandinavian apple muffins, hot from the oven; herbed eggs; a breakfast meat; sautéed potatoes; and a hot beverage. Thus fortified, guests venture forth to discover the multi-layered personality of Portsmouth, which is redolent of history and filled with diverse and exciting restaurants and shops.

LEIGHTON INN, 69 Richards Avenue, Portsmouth, NH 03801; (603) 433-2188; Catherine Stone, host. Open all year. Five rooms with 4 baths. Rates: $55 to $75 double with full New England breakfast. Well-behaved children welcome; no pets; Visa/MasterCard; French, German spoken. 1913 Steinway available, bicycles for rental. Portsmouth is an historic city with many activities, including a summer arts festival and many fine restaurants.

DIRECTIONS: from I-95 take exit 5 to Portsmouth Traffic Circle and follow Rte. 1 Bypass North to Maplewood Ave. exit and turn right. Follow Maplewood into town, where its name changes to Middle St., which makes a broad curve to the right. Richards Ave. is first left after curve; inn is 6th house on left.

A perfect room.

THE GLYNN HOUSE

Where Victoriana abounds

Back in 1895 the biggest man in town was L. W. Packard, owner of the woolen mill, and Ashland's largest employer. The new house Mr. Packard built for his family that year was everything one would expect of a man of his position.

It was Queen Anne in style, with a cupola tower and wide, gingerbread porches. The inside was finished all in carved oak and decorated with wallpapers of the period. It was indeed a fine family mansion.

Now it is home to another family—the Patermans—and their many bed and breakfast guests.

Karol Paterman is a former restaurateur from Philadelphia, but is originally from Gdansk, the home of his fellow countryman President Lech Walesa, who worked at the famous Polish shipyard there. Betsy is also a restaurateur, and a native of Philadelphia, where she met Karol.

Together with Karol's mother as housekeeper *par excellence*, they chose the rewarding life of bed and breakfast hosts a couple of years ago, when they found the Packard mansion in central New Hampshire.

As avid collectors and auction goers, furnishing the house was right up their alley. Victorian antiques abound throughout the common rooms and the four guest rooms. One guest room in the tower is oval in shape, and offers an interesting furniture arrangement which includes a canopied bed and a Jacuzzi right in the room. There is a fireplace in another guest room, with a fine mahogany bed and interesting Victorian memorabilia, a plethora of which is displayed in the other rooms as well.

A delicious, full breakfast is served, varying from day-to-day, but fresh farmers' eggs are always a staple of the dishes prepared by the exhuberant hosts.

THE GLYNN HOUSE INN, 43 Highland St., Ashland, NH 03217; (603) 968-3775; Betsy and Karol Paterman, owners. Open all year. Four guest rooms with private baths. Rates: $65 weekdays, $75 weekends, per room. Includes full breakfast of fresh farmers' eggs. Children 6 and over welcome; no pets; smoking in sitting room only; Polish and Russian spoken; Visa/Mastercard. Many fine restaurants in area, which is noted for Alpine skiing, fall foliage, and the lake and countryside seen in the film *On Golden Pond.*

DIRECTIONS: take exit 24 from I-93 onto Rte. 25/3 into Ashland and left on Highland to inn.

People love it here.

MOOSE MOUNTAIN LODGE

Casual, with lots of fireplaces

Moose Mountain Lodge virtually spills over the western slope of Moose Mountain. Porch-sitters recline in full view of unspoiled countryside, where Vermont's Green Mountains rise out of the clear, smooth-running waters of the Connecticut River.

Just seven miles northeast of Hanover, home of Dartmouth College, the lodge is a back-country hideaway on 350 acres, situated on a dirt cul de sac that ends at the top of a ridge. Between the lodge and the mountaintop the road is veined with numerous trails, far away from the whoosh of passing traffic and noisy crowds. Winter skiers and summer hikers can disappear into the woods and feel secluded.

Inside, Kay and Peter Shumway cater to nature-lovers who gather around one of three common-room fireplaces. The stone fireplace in the living room warms-up conversation as much as it does noses and toes.

"You can put your feet up here," says Kay, who emphasizes that her guests feel relaxed in the fresh, clean, and comfortable lodge.

After dinner many folks head down to the bar room (BYOB) to play ping-pong, darts, or a board game by yet another native stone fireplace, this one mottled with garnet-studded rose quartz. A working player piano livens up the evening with classic old favorites. Once the music's over, guests retire to appropriately rustic bedrooms made especially homey with handmade spruce log or other wooden beds and muted linens.

MOOSE MOUNTAIN LODGE, Etna, NH 03750; (603) 643-3529; Kay and Peter Shumway, innkeepers. Open January to late March and June to late October. Twelve cozy rooms share five modern bathrooms. Hearty breakfast. Rates: $50 per person. American plans available. Children over 5 are welcome; no pets; no smoking. 50 km of cross-country ski trails; downhill skiing within 10 miles; hiking trails. Dartmouth College offers cultural events year-round.

DIRECTIONS: from exit 18 on Rte. 89, go north on Rte. 120 toward Hanover, ½ mile. Higbea Motel and Barbelle's Restaurant are on the left. Turn right here onto Etna Rd. into Etna Village. Go ½ mile past the Etna Store (phone from here if it's your first time) and turn right onto Rudsboro Rd. (just before the church. Go up Rudsboro Rd. 2 miles, then turn left on Dana Rd. Continue on Dana Rd. for ½ mile. Turn right. Drive up the mountain one mile to the Lodge.

WHITE GOOSE INN

Cozy American with European panache

Orford is seated by the banks of the upper Connecticut River just across a bridge from Fairlee, Vermont. Originally a "fort town" built by the British, it soon hummed with activity from logging and agriculture. Seven "ridge houses" dating from between 1773 and 1839 form a stately white row by the green in the town's center.

The White Goose Inn is also celebrated for its elm tree growing through the circular colonial revival porch. Manfred and Karin Wolf adopted this brick and woodframe home and transformed it into a cozy American country classic with European panache.

Karin, a craftsperson whose work is evident throughout the inn, did all the delicate stenciling, made the pierced parchment lampshades, and cunningly assembled traveler's sewing kits for each impeccably designed, spotless guest room.

White geese are the house motif. A porcelain goose with a pink satin ribbon around its neck sits in the window; a cloth goose pokes its head out of a basket on the hutch; and an early American metal cut-out depicts a young girl followed by two geese. And there's a white wooden goose on the marble-topped treadle sewing machine base in the hall to greet guests when they arrive.

Breakfasts are very special here, reflecting the hosts' European heritage. Hearty home-baked goods look even more tempting on the Wolf's fine china.

The tasteful choices in furnishing and accessories are consistent throughout the White Goose. The parlor exudes the glow from an unusual porcelain chandelier. The dining room benefits from a beautifully crafted modern wood table and tall Shaker-style chairs.

This wonderful hideaway engages its guests, tempting them again and again to relax and sit back in an attractive setting where the details in every room please the eye.

THE WHITE GOOSE INN, Rte. 10, P.O. Box 17, Orford, NH 03777; (603) 353-4812; Manfred and Karin Wolf. German spoken. Open all year. Sixteen guest rooms, most with private baths. Rates; $75 to $160, including a full country breakfast. Children under 8 discouraged; no pets; smoking discouraged. MasterCard/Visa. Hiking, biking trails, golf, skiing, sleigh rides; Saint-Gaudens National Historic Site. Dartmouth College, 15 miles.

DIRECTIONS: from I-91, take exit 15 (Fairlee, VT); cross the bridge to New Hampshire and take Rte. 10 south one mile. The inn is on the left. From I-93, take exit for I-89 and continue to Rte. 10 north. The inn is approximately 15 miles north of Hanover on the right.

Collecting maple syrup from the inn's own trees.

THE CHASE HOUSE

A famous banker's birthplace

Born in 1808, Salmon P. Chase spent the first decade of his life in the village of Cornish, New Hampshire. By the age of eleven he was sent to Ohio to live with his uncle, an Episcopal bishop, but in time Chase returned to New Hampshire to attend Dartmouth College. Eventually he was elected to the United States Senate, and after six years was elected to two terms as Ohio's governor, after which he returned to Washington and the Senate. From there, this remarkable American went on to serve Abraham Lincoln as Secretary of the Treasury, and soon thereafter was appointed Chief Justice of the United States, where he served until his death in 1873. In his lifetime he was a tireless anti-slavery spokesman; founded the Republican Party; had his picture engraved on the $10,000 bill; and gave his name to the Chase Manhattan Bank.

Chase's birthplace, one of the finest homes in this tiny Connecticut River valley village, has been meticulously restored as a bed and breakfast inn by Peter Burling, an attorney and a member of Cornish's town planning board. He commissioned the talents of experienced restoration experts, who thoroughly and carefully pieced together the checkered history of the house.

The result is a stunning, early Federal house that sits on the banks of the river, surrounded by stately shade trees. The furnishings throughout are elegant, comfortable, and simple, and they enhance one's enjoyment of the home's lovely architectural detail.

The full breakfast that is served each morning prepares one for exploring the wooded New England countryside. The Chase House is centrally located nearby Hanover and Dartmouth College, as well as the sophisticated shops and restaurants of Woodstock, Vermont.

THE CHASE HOUSE, RR 2, Box 909, Cornish, NH 03745; (603) 675-5391; Hal and Marilyn Wallace, Pete Burling, hosts. Open all year. Six rooms, 5 with private baths, 1 sharing. Rates: $75 to $95, with full breakfast; weekend discounts. Enquire about children; no pets; Visa/MasterCard. Canoeing, hiking, cross-country skiing on premises. Interesting dining in area.

DIRECTIONS: from I-91 take Ascutney exit 8 across Connecticut River, turn north on Rte. 12A for 4 miles to inn.

High ceilings make for grand spaces.

CRAB APPLE INN

With an English country garden

Crab Apple Inn is charming—from its well-preserved doorway fan to its babbling brook. White trim and black shutters complement the 1835 brick Federal building and the white picket fence that encloses the tidy house and its brilliantly colored English country garden.

Two cheery third-floor rooms boast the best view, overlooking most of the inn's two-and-a-half acres and Crosby Mountain. Yet every guest gets something special: an arched canopy bed, a hand-carved sleigh bed, a brass bed. Intimate and cozy, the household harbors a warmth that emanates primarily from its two owners, Carolyn and Bill Crenson, who had been planning to open a bed and breakfast for years.

An award-winning sign.

The inn's library offers a variety of periodicals and books, and all the public rooms are tastefully furnished in a traditional style.

This is indeed snow country, the gateway to the White Mountains. Polar Caves is one mile down the road, and Waterville Valley and Tenney Mountain, minutes away.

Warm weather enthusiasts can wade in nearby Newfound Lake or relax on the brick patio, sipping iced tea by the French doors, with candy and fresh fruit available. Breakfasts, whether indoors or *al fresco*, feature refreshingly simple, home-cooked country fare.

Carolyn and Bill attend to the small details that make life more enjoyable when on the road—leaving terry cloth robes for those guests in rooms with shared baths and offering wine or tea and snacks in the afternoon.

CRAB APPLE INN, Rte. 25, RR 4, Box 1955, Plymouth, NH 03264; (603) 536-4476; Carolyn and Bill Crenson, innkeepers. Open all year. Two suites (Queen beds), two guestrooms, all with private baths. Rates: $70 to $85, including a country breakfast. Children over 8 welcome; no pets; limited smoking; MasterCard/Visa. All-season recreation in area; antiquing. Good restaurants nearby.

DIRECTIONS: from I-93, take exit 26 and head west on Rte. 25. The inn is 4 miles from the interstate on the left.

". . . and the snow lay round about, deep and crisp and even."

HAVERHILL INN

1810 Federal house near village green

In its heyday, Haverhill was a county seat, and prosperity left its mark in the form of grand mansions, many sitting high on the rise overlooking the lovely Connecticut River and Vermont's rolling hills. When the railroad bypassed Haverhill, the town stood still. Today you can't find a grocery, drug store, or even a general store. "Modernization" has never touched this island of beauty, and Haverhill is richer for its loss.

The Haverhill Inn is one of those elegantly proportioned mansions that overlooks the river. It emanates a calm and tranquility that speaks well of its keeper, Stephen Campbell. But this peaceful atmosphere can also be traced to older inhabitants. Three volumes of data and letters have been compiled on the history of Haverhill and the house. Tracing its lineage, readers discover that each owner bestowed genuine love on this home. This fortunate history has left its mark.

Today the inn comprises four guest rooms. Each is spacious and each has a working fireplace. The living room, with its upright piano, is a comfortable gathering spot, where guests can enjoy a glass of sherry, cup of tea, or a good read.

Stephen has a thriving career as a computer programming consultant, in addition to innkeeping. Since most of his work is done at home, the inn is always well tended. As a dedicated and gifted cook Stephen makes breakfast a very special event, especially on Sunday.

Haverhill Inn is now part of a popular summer canoeing inn-to-inn trip.

HAVERHILL INN , Dartmouth College Hwy., Rte. 10, Haverhill, NH 03765; (603) 989-5961; Stephen Campbell, host. 1810 Federal style house on quiet street near village green. Open June through Feb. Four guest rooms, all private baths. Rates: $50 single, $75 double, with $10 per additional occupant, including full breakfast. Afternoon tea and coffee. Restaurants nearby. Older children welcome; pets discouraged; smoking restricted; no credit cards.

DIRECTIONS: from Hanover, take Rte. 10 North 27 miles. From NYC (6 hrs.), take I-91 North to exit 15 (Fairlee, Vt.), cross river to Orford, N.H., and proceed north on Rte. 10. From Boston, I-93 to Plymouth, Rte. 25 west to Haverhill.

AMOS A. PARKER HOUSE

The place to get away from it all

If wandering off the beaten track is your idea of the perfect getaway, the southwest corner of New Hampshire beckons. Visitors to the area come to escape the rat race and to get in touch with life's essentials. The area is richly blessed with sparkling lakes, ponds, and streams; groves of rhododendron that burst into bloom each summer; and maple trees that glow in the autumn and produce sweet syrup in early spring. The region is dominated by Mount Monadnock, which over the years has inspired such artists as Emerson, Kipling, and Kilmer. Thoreau climbed to the summit three times, and the mountain was a constant companion during his solitary sojourn on Walden Pond.

Such relaxed and gentle surroundings are complemented by the historic Amos A. Parker House.

The Great Room, so-named because everyone exclaims, "What a great room!" when they first see it.

A stay at this colonial bed and breakfast inn is like visiting a favorite relative. Innkeeper Freda Houpt is the inn's genial host and she makes visitors feel a part of this fine old place. The earliest section of the house dates back to the mid-1700s, with an addition built in 1780. Freda has filled her home with comfortable furnishings that match the Federal period, museum quality orientals, and antiques. She is justifiably proud of her gardens and her lawn, which sweeps gently to an active beaver pond at the edge of the grass.

Besides the natural beauty of the area, visitors enjoy cultural events, such as plays and concerts, offered throughout the year. Also, the village of Fitzwilliam (which, for trivia buffs, is the only town in the United States bearing that name), as well as the surrounding countryside, is well-known for the quality of its antiques and crafts shops.

AMOS A. PARKER HOUSE, Box 202, Rte. 119, Fitzwilliam, NH 03447; (603) 585-6540; Freda B. Houpt, proprietor. Open all year. Five rooms, 3 with private baths. Rates: $55 to $80 with full breakfast. Children over 10 welcome; no pets; no credit cards. Canoeing, golf, tennis, hiking, biking, climbing in area. Country inn dining nearby.

DIRECTIONS: from I-91 take exit 28A to Rte. 10 North to Rte. 119 East. From Boston take Rte. 2 West to Rte. 140 North to Rte. 12 North to Rte. 119 West.

BENJAMIN PRESCOTT INN

American history

Built as a hostelry by Colonel Benjamin Prescott, a hero of the Battle of Bunker Hill, this inn is a footnote in the pages of American history. Each room bears the name of a Prescott family member.

Barry and Jan Miller have comfortably furnished the inn and filled it with all manner of interesting collectibles. Barry inherited his grandfather's collection of sand from around the world, and there are ship models (assembled by Barry) including the *Eagle*, an 1850s Maine schooner. Also displayed are framed groupings of vintage postcards, as well as rug beaters, trolley tokens, and antique children's clothing arranged like a Smithsonian exhibit.

The John Adams attic suite on the third floor is well worth the steep climb. Its spacious bedchamber, with two built-in sleeping alcoves and adjoining sitting room (with kitchen, stereo facilities, and scenic balcony), are fashioned out of fantasy.

What the hosts have not been able to do is create the setting, but beautiful New Hampshire provides that. The house backs out onto a vast seven-hundred acre pastoral dairy farm with a view of the farmer driving his hay wagon to and from the barn.

Cross-country and alpine skiing are minutes away, and the renowned Peterborough Players perform top-rated summer stock. Historic Jaffrey Center is a delightful colonial village brimming with history.

Barry, formerly a hotel manager, is the perfect host. And Jan's bedside chocolate truffles cannot be described in mere words.

THE BENJAMIN PRESCOTT INN, Rte. 124, Jaffrey, NH 03452; (603) 532-6637; Barry and Janice Miller, owners. Open all year. Ten rooms, including 2 suites, all with private baths. Rates: $60 to $130 per room or suite, including full breakfast. Children 10 and over welcome; no pets; smoking in common rooms only; Visa/MasterCard/American Express. Recommended dining at LataCarta, Boiler House, Del Rossi. The Cathedral of the Pines is a scenic and spiritual wonder just 2½ miles from inn.

DIRECTIONS: on Rte. 124 east of Jaffrey 2.3 miles.

All the rooms are different.

BEAL HOUSE INN

Candlelit breakfasts

Ann and Jim Carver, proprietors of this "living antique shop" bed and breakfast establishment came to this venture with three talented sons; one who restores and upholsters the furniture, one with a degree in hotel management, and one who lends general support and good cheer. In short this is a family operation of grand proportions.

Built in 1833, the Beal House Inn began as a Federal Renaissance farmhouse. Over the years, the house and barn slowly grew together, connecting through the carriage house. The five-stall horse barn became an antiques shop and thus began the tradition for providing travelers with warm New England hospitality and newfound treasures.

Each of the fourteen rooms in this hostelry has its own character—canopied, brass, spool, and four poster beds; hooked and braided rugs; comfortable wing chairs. Everything you look at, sleep atop, sit in, or admire is for sale. What better way to shop for a bed or chair than to live with it for a time. An antiques shop/inn makes for an everchanging setting, since a room that loses its elaborate Victorian canopied bed might in turn gain a weighty sleigh bed or a pair of simple pencil post twins.

Breakfast is a delightful experience in a candlelit dining room where long tables are set with Blue Willow plates on lovely antique red tablecloths. Hot popovers, the inn's specialty, begins the meal, with a large selection of fruit juices, homemade breads, and beverages following. French toast, creamy scrambled eggs served in white glass hens-on-nests, ham, bacon and fresh ground sausage are served à la carte.

The parlor features games, books, stereo views, and a fireplace. And the second floor has an inviting book-nook and a deck that reaches out to the back lawn and the terraced woods.

THE BEAL HOUSE INN, Main St., Littleton, NH 03561; (603) 444-2661; the Carver family, hosts. Frame Federal-style house has been inn-*cum*-antiques-shop for over 50 years. Open all year. Fourteen guest rooms, twelve with private baths. Rates $35 to $120, including suites, according to season and amenities. Continental breakfast included; additional charge for full country breakfast served tavern-style. Evening tea and snacks. Current menus and reservation service for local dining. Children eight and over welcome; pet boarding nearby; smoking restricted; major credit cards.

DIRECTIONS: from I-93, take exit 41 into Littleton. Turn left onto Main St. to inn, at junction of Rtes. 18 and 302.

Left, the staircase leading to the guest rooms is bedecked with whimsical bookends and doorstops.

Left, A prize music box and quilt combined in the sitting room. Above, the inn and the famous old barn that is used for many activities.

THATCHER HILL INN

Rural hospitality

This is the bed and breakfast haven of Marge and Cal Gage, who bought the property from distant relatives some years ago as a vacation home. However, with Cal nearing his retirement from the advertising business in Chicago, they decided to convert the many-bedroomed farmhouse into a bed and breakfast.

Marge took courses in hotel and restaurant man-

agement, and they moved Cal's thirty-year-old collection of furniture-sized music boxes to New Hampshire, along with their other antiques. Marge made traditional decorative quilts for all the beds, in addition to the antique quilts that are displayed as wall-hangings. Every room is papered and furnished with loving attention, and the wide boards of the original pumpkin-pine floors are polished and waxed to a beautiful satiny finish.

On the second floor, there is a large sitting room with a working fireplace. This room is available as a suite with two adjoining bedrooms and a balcony that looks out on the barn and green fields. There are three other working fireplaces in the breakfast room, sitting room, and guest room number five. As the inn is open all year, a cheery blaze on the hearth adds welcome warmth to New Hampshire's snowy winters.

THATCHER HILL INN, Thatcher Hill Road, Marlborough, NH 03455; (603) 876-3361; Marge and Cal Gage, owners. Open all year (closed occasionally in Nov., Dec., Mar., April). Seven guest rooms with private baths and 1 with working fireplace. Rates: $68 to $88 per room, including full breakfast. Children 6 and over welcome; no pets; no smoking; Visa/MasterCard. Dining and shopping in the charming nearby university town of Keene, which is also noted for its Christmas festivities.

DIRECTIONS: from I-91 take Rte. 9 west through Keene onto Rte. 101 through Marlborough to junction with Rte. 124 and right through woods for several miles to Thatcher Hill Rd. Take right to inn.

VERMONT

Left, the luxuriously furnished guest rooms are brilliantly decorated. Above, the main house.

SWIFT HOUSE INN

Genuinely luxurious

Swift House is sited impressively in a park-like setting of sweeping lawns, stately trees, and colorful flower gardens.

The entire main floor houses fruitwood-paneled reception rooms for guests' use. There is a formal sitting room, relaxing parlor, intimate bar, and an inviting screened-in porch—light and airy with white wicker furnishings—that looks out on the spacious grounds.

Five guest rooms on the second floor are superbly furnished, each being more inviting than the last. The Addison Room is decorated in pink and white wallpaper, with white wicker furniture and an ornate white iron bed. But then the Swift Room has a lovely canopied bed, and a huge bathroom with a claw-footed tub, separate stall shower, and private sun deck.

All this, however, describes only one third of the inn. Though everyone eats breakfast at the main house, across the street is the Gate House, with another five luxurious guest rooms and sitting rooms of its own. And beyond the circular driveway is the Carriage House, which was recently renovated into five guest rooms and aromatic cedar sauna, steam room, and showers.

Andrea and John Nelson bought the estate in 1985, with plans to convert it to an inn. Their consummate taste prevails throughout, and they have proven themselves masters of the ancient and noble art of innkeeping.

The previous owner was the daughter of John W. Stewart, a former Governor of Vermont, who bought the original house in 1875 from its builder, Judge Samuel Swift. Stewart's daughter lived there for 105 years, until her death in 1981 at the age of 110.

SWIFT HOUSE INN AND GATEHOUSE, 25 Stewart Lane, Middlebury, VT 05753; (802) 388-9925; Andrea and John Nelson, owners. Open all year. Fifteen guest rooms in Swift House and Gate House and 5 rooms in Carriage House, all with private baths. Rates: $65 to $185 per room, including full breakfast. Children welcome; no pets; smoking allowed; Visa/MasterCard/American Express/Discover. Middlebury is a charming Vermont college town well worth the visit.

DIRECTIONS: from south stay on Rte. 7 through Middlebury past Middlebury Inn a few blocks and turn right on Stewart Lane, which intersects Rte. 7 near Mobil station.

SHOREHAM INN AND COUNTRY STORE

A tiny town on Lake Champlain

Surrounded by apple orchards and dairy farms, and bordered on one side by Lake Champlain's sinuous tail, the Shoreham Inn and its adjoining Country Store form the heart of tiny Shoreham, Vermont. The inn's atmosphere, reflecting its beautiful setting and kind proprietors, is warm, gentle, and welcoming.

Built in 1799 as a public house, it allows today's inngoers to walk the same wooden floorboards that its first visitors trod. These wide planks are partially hidden by lustrous old area rugs and an irregular collection of antiques—none matches, but all work together—that please the eye and comfort the spirit.

Cleo and Fred Alter love original art, a taste fully developed during the days they worked together in printing and graphic design, and they exercise this love by showing the work of gifted local artists. Not a gallery per se, the inn doesn't sell work but the Alters do take pleasure in sharing beautiful things with others.

Breakfast is low-keyed. On each table guests find a canning jar filled with granola, pitchers of milk and juice, local honey and preserves, muffins or scones, and cheese. Since this is apple country, Cleo always serves the fruit in one form or another. Glass cookie jars in the center of each large dining table are always stocked with homebaked sweets for snackers.

The Country Store, just next to the inn, supplies everything from magazines and groceries to hardware and wine. The Alters operate a small delicatessen in back, where you can order a pizza or sandwiches and salads. Picnic tables on the village green beckon on a summer day.

SHOREHAM INN AND COUNTRY STORE, Shoreham, VT 05770; (802) 897-5081; Cleo and Fred Alter, hosts. Built as an inn in 1799, the Shoreham served as a way station for floating railroad bridge and ferry across Lake Champlain. Open all year. Eleven guest rooms, some accommodating four people, shared baths. Rates: $40 single, $70 double, including country breakfast. Numerous restaurants in area. Children welcome; no pets; no credit cards. Area offers aquatic and other sports, museums, Ft. Ticonderoga, Morgan horse farm. Daily boat trips on lake.

DIRECTIONS: inn is 12 miles southwest of Middlebury. Follow Rte. 22A from Fairhaven to Rte. 74 west. From Burlington, take 7 south to 22A at Vergennes, then take 74 west into Shoreham. Ticonderoga ferry operates to and from Shoreham.

SOUTH SHIRE INN

Special comfort and personality

Bennington, Vermont is a bustling New England village, tucked securely in a broad and handsome Green Mountain valley. The South Shire Inn, which sits at the edge of the handsome residential district, is perfectly situated between historic Old Bennington, with its famous Battle Monument, Old First Church, and Old Burying Ground (resting place of poet Robert Frost) and the shops and restaurants that cluster at the village center.

The house dates back to the late 1800s, when Bennington's prominent Graves family built a compound of five adjoining mansions to accommodate the burgeoning clan. No expense was spared when they raised Louis Graves' Queen Anne Victorian home, and today this solid and spacious mansion serves as contemporary Bennington's finest bed and breakfast inn.

Owned and operated by Francoise von Trapp, the South Shire Inn is striking and handsome. Of special note on the first floor is the very grand library, paneled with lustrous Honduran mahogany and outfitted with a working, tile-faced fireplace and built-in, leaded glass bookcases. The adjoining breakfast room is so encrusted with rococo plaster friezes it could put a wedding cake to shame.

One bedroom is found on the inn's first floor and the remainder are located upstairs, on the second and third floors. Each has its own special comfort and personality. Several spacious chambers come complete with working fireplaces.

Great care and thought went into restoring and furnishing the inn, which adds to the sense of solidity and "rightness" about the place. The turn-of-the-century carriage barn has recently been renovated into luxurious guest rooms, with fireplaces and Jacuzzi baths.

THE SOUTH SHIRE INN, 124 Elm Street, Bennington, VT 05201; (802) 447-3839; Francoise von Trapp and Laurie Beth Ayers, hosts. Open all year. Nine rooms with private baths. Rates: $90 to $135, varying seasonally. Children over 10 welcome; no pets; Visa/MasterCard/American Express. State-of-the-art facilities available for conferences. Fishing, golf, hiking, antiquing, museums, outlet stores in area. Many restaurants for dining.

DIRECTIONS: take Elm St. off Rte. 7 between Jefferson and Dewey.

The back garden, where Norman Rockwell's studio is located.

THE INN ON COVERED BRIDGE GREEN

Norman Rockwell slept here

Norman Rockwell came to Arlington, Vermont, when he was forty-six years old, inspired by the beautiful countryside and the people who lived there—of whom he said ". . . the sincere, honest, homespun types that I love to paint." From 1941 to 1954, he lived in the house that is now The Inn on Covered Bridge, painting his war-years pictures in the studio behind. *The Country Doctor, Christmas Homecoming, First Day at School* were among these paintings, and many of the townsfolk were his models.

Anne and Rob Weber, Americans who lived in England, and later in a Scottish castle, have bought and assumed stewardship of the Rockwell house. They brought sets of antique furniture, armoires, washstands, and carpets from Europe to furnish the two-hundred-year-old farmhouse, where Rockwell's visitors included his good friend, Grandma Moses.

Across the way from the inn's front porch is the grassy lawn where Ethan Allen drilled his Green Mountain Boys, whom he led in the surprise attack to capture the British-held Fort Ticonderoga. There is a pavilion on the green, where Rockwell and his neighbors danced on Saturday night, and beyond that, a classic Vermont covered bridge from which the inn takes its name.

Nearby flows the Batten Kill River, one of America's finest trout streams. A stroll along River Road provides panoramic views of neighboring farms and meadows, and there are superb hiking trails on Stratton Mountain. Three of the finest summer stock theaters are just a half hour away as is *Hildene,* Robert Todd Lincoln's estate.

A gallery housed in an historic Arlington church displays Rockwell's *Saturday Evening Post* covers, illustrations, and ads. You get the uncanny feeling that people you see there today—at the gas station, at the general store, in the churchyard—are the very same people he drew for magazine covers a generation ago.

THE INN ON COVERED BRIDGE GREEN, RD 1, Box 3550, Arlington, VT 05250; (800) 726-9480, (802) 375-9489; Anne and Ron Weber, owners. Open all year. Five guest rooms in inn plus Norman Rockwell's studio in garden, all with private baths. Rates: $60 for single, $125 doubles, $170 studio (sleeps 7). Includes full breakfast. Well-mannered children welcome; no pets; no smoking; no credit cards. Excellent dining in Arlington and East Arlington.

DIRECTIONS: from Rte. 7 in Arlington take Rte. 313 west at Arlington Inn 4½ miles to red covered bridge.

The Josephine Room is exquisitely detailed.

THE JACKSON HOUSE AT WOODSTOCK

Elegant décor

The one hundred-year-old Jackson House is as friendly and warm as it is elegant. Although it has hosted travelers for the last fifty years, it was only in 1984 that it became one of the most exquisitely furnished inns in Vermont, when Bruce McIlveen and Jack Foster took it in hand.

With consummate taste and the sensitive appreciation of connoisseurs, they have created ten guest rooms, each singularly fashioned, and all a memorable experience for guests.

We can mention only a few, the first being the Gloria Swanson Room, named after her because she stayed there. It is all done in birds-eye and curly maple—floors, bedstead, picture frames, and furniture—with a lemon, green, and white color scheme. The Mary T. Lincoln Room is High Victorian, with a great carved double bed, and an ornately tufted, green-upholstered occasional chair.

A full breakfast is served, and the menu changes daily, but could consist of fresh fruit compôte with peach schnapps, Santa Fe omelets, rosemary potatoes, broccoli with hollandaise, and homemade scones and muffins.

THE JACKSON HOUSE AT WOODSTOCK, Rte. 4 West, Woodstock, VT 05091; (802) 457-2065; Jack D. Foster and Bruce McIlveen, hosts. Closed April 1 to May 15 and November 1 to December 15. Ten guest rooms, each with private bath. Rates: $120, $130, $155 double. Children over 14 welcome; no pets; no smoking; no credit cards. Robert Trent Jones golf course, tennis in area. French touring bikes available.

DIRECTIONS: The Jackson House is 1½ miles west of Woodstock Village on Rte. 4

SHIRE INN

Where guests come to relax

One hour from Burlington and halfway between Boston and Montreal, the Shire Inn affords comfort and elegant surroundings for guests traveling through central Vermont.

Love at first sight was the reason the Papas bought the inn. Enclosed by a white picket fence, the house is constructed of handsome Vermont brick with a granite arch curving gracefully over its front door. Spring and summer gardens add color and fragrance; a wooden bridge stands behind the inn and the White River flows past it.

Six distinct guest rooms, all named for counties in Vermont, are furnished with period antiques. Four of them have working fireplaces. All of the bedsteads are dressed with country bedspreads and ample comforters and a generous supply of books and magazines is provided in all rooms.

A sumptuous full breakfast is served. Favorite entrées include a cream cheese omelet topped with mint, every manner of pancake, including the house specialty, an Eierkuchen spread with an apricot sauce, and baked fruit. Dinners are served during the week by reservation. A minimum two-night weekend includes one five-course dinner which might feature pork chops with caraway stuffing, fillet of sole in wine, chicken in a spice or curry sauce, or swordfish with lime mayonnaise.

Cross-country skiing in Chelsea, downhill skiing in Barnard, swimming and boating on Lake Fairlee, theater, art galleries, and restaurants in nearby Woodstock and Montpelier make the Shire an inn for all seasons.

THE SHIRE INN, P.O. Box 37, Main St., Chelsea, VT 05038; (802) 685-3031; James and Mary Lee Papa, innkeepers. Open all year. Federal-style brick house built in 1832. Six guest rooms, all with private baths, four with working fireplaces. Rates: $70 to $88 double depending upon season. MAP $130 to $165. Delicious full breakfast included. Minimum two night weekend including one dinner. Children over 6 welcome; no pets; no smoking; Visa/MasterCard. Cross-country skiing (skis available at no extra charge), hiking, antiquing.

DIRECTIONS: from I-89 take the Sharon exit (exit 2) to Rte. 14 to S. Royalton, to Rte. 110 north to Chelsea. From I-91, take the Thetford exit (exit 14) to Rte. 113 north to Chelsea. The inn is on the village's main road, on the left.

Wonderful hosts in the back country

The Parmenter House is a back-country hiker's dream. Dirt roads and paths around Belmont include trail heads for the Long and Appalachian trails, and there are at least ten day-hike segments within half an hour of the house including a trek to an herb farm; along Towner Road (the most photographed road in Vermont); and to a music camp that offers classical concerts.

Gazing at Belmont's scenic countryside, it's hard to believe that the town once depended on its factories and was called Mechanicsville. When the railroad came through, the town was renamed Belmont.

Guests often take breakfast on the deck out back. Afternoon tea is served in the Eastlake-inspired living room, amid paintings and screens, attractive turn-of-the-century furnishings, and the elegant wallpaper of Bradbury and Bradbury.

THE PARMENTER HOUSE, P.O. Box 106, Belmont, VT 05730; (802) 259-2009; Cynthia and Lester Firschein, hosts. Spanish and French spoken. Open all year. Five guest rooms, each with private bath. Rates: $65 to $95; additional person, $15. Includes continental breakfast. MasterCard/Visa for deposits only. Theater, many outdoor activities, Ludlow restaurants nearby.

DIRECTIONS: from I-91, take exit 6 and then Rte. 103 through Chester and Ludlow. After Ludlow center and Okemo Access Road (which will be on left), stay on Rte. 103 until you come to a blinking light. Turn left at this light. After two miles you will come to the center of Belmont, marked by a four-cornered intersection. Turn left; the Parmenter House is the second house on your left, directly opposite the white church.

A classic farmhouse in western Vermont

The emerald hills of western Vermont are dappled with lush farm fields, picturesque orchards, and crystal lakes, and the Maplewood Inn is nestled in the heart of this natural paradise. The inn is a classic New England farmhouse—its clapboards painted sparkling white with colonial red doors and shutters. Each morning a full breakfast—including freshly baked breads, fresh fruit, Belgian waffles, eggs Florentine, quiche, and hot beverages—is served.

The décor of the inn conforms to a country motif. Each bedroom is fresh and comfortable. Two second-floor suites are particularly spacious, each having a private sitting room, and the only guest room on the main floor has its own entrance.

MAPLEWOOD INN, Rte. 22A South, RR1 Box 4460, Fair Haven, VT 05743; (802) 265-8039; Cindy Soder, host. Open all year. Three rooms with private and shared baths and 2 suites with private baths. Rates: $65 to $95 with breakfast. Children over 6 with prior approval; no pets; Visa/MasterCard/American Express. Croquet and lawn games on premises and water skiing, boating, fishing, hiking, riding, and golfing nearby. Country inn dining in nearby inns.

DIRECTIONS: from Vermont Rte. 4 take Rte. 22A South through Fair Haven for 1 mile. Inn is on the left.

1811 HOUSE

An upscale inn with a pub

For almost a century-and-a-half, Manchester has flourished as a vacation place and spa. Early visitors found its inns, taverns, beautiful countryside, and four miles of marble sidewalks a welcome escape from the city. Mary Todd Lincoln came here to rest from the tensions of the Civil War.

Franklin Orvis, a key figure in Manchester's growth, was an early hosteler and part of his original home is incorporated into the Equinox Hotel—a sprawling resort with a spa and golf course. The back of the 1811 House, with its magnificently tended flower gardens, looks out on the Equinox golf course and Bromley Mountain.

This is not just another inn. The groomed and elegant 1811 House is impeccable inside and out. An historic building, it is ideally situated next to the classic New England-spired church on the equally classic Manchester village green.

All of the rooms in the house are simple and lovely. The first-floor parlors and dining room are furnished with a collection of fine English antiques, crystal, and paintings of country scenes. Each of

A second floor guest room.

the ten bedrooms has a private bath, sports its own color scheme, and exudes its own personality.

In the center of the building there is an English pub with dartboard and fireplace. This fits well with Bruce Duff's passion for wine, and he is the consummate bar tender—an oenophile who metes out his superb wines measure-for-measure with his knowledge of the grape. Gardening, his other love, has bloomed in the terraced gardens, which overwhelm the senses with their color and fragrance.

Marny, who used to teach cooking, enjoys preparing a full gourmet breakfast that might include eggs Benedict, grilled mushrooms, succulent ham, bacon, scones, and an endless variety of pancakes. Along with freshly-squeezed juice or fresh fruit, the fare is presented on fine china and crystal.

These are special innkeepers who love sharing their passions with those lucky enough to be their guests.

1811 HOUSE , Manchester Village, VT 05254; (802) 362-1811; Bruce and Marny Duff, innkeepers. Excellent example of Federal architecture, which was long a famous summer resort in the 1800s. Open year-round. Ten guest rooms, private baths. Rates: $100 to $170 double. Full sit-down breakfast. No children under sixteen; no pets; major credit cards. Excellent dining in the area and occasional dinners served on premises for guests. Hiking, fishing, tennis, golf, swimming, antiquing, winter skiing.

DIRECTIONS: from Bennington, Vt., drive north on historic Rte. 7A. Inn is in Manchester Village on the green, next to the Congregational Church (with spire).

A gorgeous stone house in a park-like Vermont setting.

GREYSTONE

Rustic charm in horse country

Once a shoe factory, Connie Miller transformed this 1830 stone house into a charming bed and breakfast, with lilac bushes and lavender plantings in front. Just down the way is the main street of Reading, with its library, school, town hall, church, and farmers' market—a picture-postcard town of six hundred souls.

This is horse country, home to the venerable Green Mountain Horse Association, and people from all over descend upon this area to ride. It is commonplace to see riders on the country roads, trails, and mountain tops. Ms. Miller herself is a seasoned rider, and her riding boots, and at times her saddle, are in the entryway of the house.

The Greystone's guest rooms are charming. One has a peach floral canopied bed with matching wallpaper and drapes. Another is papered in blue flowers, has a sitting room, and overlooks a mani-cured lawn and gentle mountains. The third floor suite has wide floorboards, comfortable furnishings, skylights—and is a bit closer to heaven. All of the furnishings are Connie's, gathered on trips and from "past lives." There are also personal keepsakes, including drawings and photos of horses and riders, and an old sepia photograph of Connie as a child on her very first ride.

The parlor is warm and inviting, with its wood-burning stove, yellow wainscoting, blue trim, and floral wallpaper. Cows at a nearby dairy farm may be glimpsed from the parlor windows, and in autumn each window reveals a kaleidoscope of fall colors.

For non-riding spouses or friends, there is fishing on the grounds and swimming at a local swimming hole. There are plenty of antiques shops and auctions, and the town of Woodstock, with its restaurants and shops, is just a short distance away. Facilities at the Woodstock Inn include tennis courts, a pool, and an eighteen-hole golf course.

GREYSTONE, RR 1, Box 85, Reading, VT 05062; (802) 484-7200; Constance Hughes Miller, owner. Open all year. Two guest rooms sharing sumptuous bath and one suite with private bath. Rates: $65 to $120 double, including full breakfast. Enquire about children; no pets; smoking in reception rooms only; a little Spanish spoken; no credit cards (personal checks accepted). Fine gourmet dining down the road at Kedron Valley Inn.

DIRECTIONS: off I-91 on Rte. 106, between Reading and South Woodstock. Call for directions.

The wood paneled staircase, laden with teddy bears.

HUGGING BEAR INN

The healing power of Teddy Bears

The warm spirit of the Hugging Bear embraces one and all who pass through its doors. Georgette Thomas came to innkeeping from a caring career as a counselor with a degree in social work. When she discovered an article in *Prevention* magazine touting the healing power of teddy bears, she knew she had found the perfect theme for this rambling, Queen Anne Victorian bed and breakfast inn, which sits on the main street of historic Chester, Vermont.

Teddy bears are found in every nook and cranny of the inn. They play the piano, peek out from potted plants, climb the lovely Victorian staircase, and perch atop each bed. Besides the inn, the Hugging Bear Shoppe, located in the back, is dedicated to the irresistible charms of the teddy bear.

Georgette's son, Paul, a wildlife artist and sculptor, and his wife, Diane, help out with the innkeeping. Because the Thomases are sensitive to the difficulties of parents traveling with children, they welcome families with open arms. Children are encouraged to choose the teddy bears of their choice to sleep with at night, and occasionally they may borrow favorites from the shop, as long as they promise to return them "to work" by 8 A.M. But it isn't strictly children who are moved by this colorful menagerie of huggable creatures. The Thomases report that a majority of adults who pass through their inn fall under the spell of teddy bear power.

THE HUGGING BEAR INN & SHOPPE, Main Street, Box 32, Chester, VT 05143; (802) 875-2412; Georgette, Paul, and Diane Thomas, hosts. Open all year. Six rooms with private baths. Rates: $55–$65 single, $70–$95 double, children under 14 $10, over 14 $20 extra, with full breakfast and afternoon cheese, crackers, and cider. Children welcome; pets limited; no smoking; all credit cards accepted. Four-room bear shop. Hugging teddy bears encouraged. Badminton, volleyball, croquet on premises. Antiquing, flea markets, auctions, biking, golf, tennis, and skiing nearby. A special event occurs on the second weekend of December, when the town celebrates a Victorian Christmas. Lighting trees, caroling, and wearing Victorian costumes are among the colorful activities. The inn provides period costumes for guests to wear to a reception for Santa Claus, who arrives in a horse drawn carriage or sled, snow permitting.

DIRECTIONS: located on the main street of Chester, Vermont.

CHARLES A. PARKER PHOTOGRAPH

QUECHEE BED & BREAKFAST

Overlooking the Quechee Gorge

From the bunches of dried herbs and flowers hanging from the rafters, to the stencilled curtains, braided rugs, and hand-crafted wreaths, Susan Kaduboski has recreated an album of rooms from the pages of *Country Living*.

The Kaduboskis rescued an old post-and-beam colonial farm house and turned it into a charming bed and breakfast that resounds with special touches: a vintage sled coffee table festooned with plants, a graceful tapestry couch, plenty of family treasures, and an abundant dose of floral motifs.

Entering the house from the front, you can hardly anticipate the awesome view that awaits you. From windows at the rear of the inn, you suddenly discover that you are perched atop the Quechee Gorge, so aptly dubbed the "Grand Canyon of the East."

Left, top, a waterside table overlooks the rushing falls at the Simon Pearce restaurant in Quechee; bottom, one of the inn's impeccably decorated guest rooms.

Outdoor tables and chairs provide excellent vantage points for viewing this beautiful section of the Ottaquechee River.

Guest rooms are all singular, with an assortment of pretty wallpapers, rice-carved four-posters, and sleigh beds on wide pine floorboards or hardwood floors. Some of the rooms offer spectacular views. Although the inn is on Route 4, hemlocks and woodpiles are useful as baffling, and colorful flower beds lap up to the windows.

The guest book is filled with rave reviews about the food served in the charming breakfast room. Perfectly scrambled eggs with chives, Vermont smoked meats, waffles done to a turn, and Susan's special French toast seem to be favorites.

You can walk over a covered bridge to the village of Quechee in a matter of minutes. Be sure to visit Simon Pearce, a mill converted into a store and restaurant, where you can shop for tableware, enjoy a meal, and watch glass-blowing artisans.

QUECHEE BED & BREAKFAST, 753 Woodstock Rd. (Rte. 4), P.O. Box 0080, Quechee, VT 05059; (802) 295-1776; Susan and Ken Kaduboski, owners. Open all year. Eight guest rooms with private baths. Rates: $85 to $125 per room, including full breakfast. No children; no pets; smoking allowed except in breakfast room; Spanish spoken; Visa/MasterCard. Overlooks town of Quechee, with its shops, restaurants, crafts center, and glass works; nearby to Woodstock, one of America's most charming upscale villages.

DIRECTIONS: from west, exit 1 off I-89 to Rte. 4 west for 4½ miles. Watch for sign on right.

MASSACHUSETTS

NORTHFIELD COUNTRY HOUSE

A well-kept secret revealed

Hidden in the hills of the beautiful Connecticut River Valley, Northfield Country House is one of those special places that visitors hope to keep a secret, all to themselves.

The aura of romance begins as you wind your way up the drive. Trees suddenly part to reveal a gracefully proportioned English manor house built in 1901 by a wealthy Boston shipbuilder who had an eye for beauty and the purse to pursue it. He insisted upon the finest handcarved cherry wainscoting, mantels, and doors; a broad staircase; leaded glass windows; and a twelve-foot stone hearth in which is embedded the message, "Love Warms The Heart As Fire The Hearth."

Andrea Dale's country house has been decorated with an eye to combining design and color into an art form. The living room with its stone hearth and three plush and generous couches invites quiet relaxation and easy conversation.

The house offers the comforts of home plus special extras—pretty sitting areas in all of the guest rooms, rich Bokara and Herziz carpets to cushion the foot. A romantic hideaway with working fireplace, velvet settee, and thick comforter on an antique bed feels rich and warm; another blue and white chamber complete with brass and iron bedstead and white wicker armchair is crisp, fresh, and old-fashioned.

Breakfast, which is served on the porch in the summer and in the cherry-paneled dining room when the weather is wet or cold, is simply splendid, with popovers and cheese and mushroom omelets the popular fare.

NORTHFIELD COUNTRY HOUSE, School St., Northfield, MA 01360; (413) 498-2692; Andrea Dale, owner. English manor house set on 16 acres. Open year-round. Seven guest rooms, shared baths. Rates: $50 to $90. Full breakfast served daily. Children 10 and over; no pets; Visa/MasterCard; checks accepted.

DIRECTIONS: take I-91 to Exit 28A. Follow Rte. 10 north to Northfield Center. School St. is in center of town, at the firehouse. Turn at firehouse and drive 9/10 of a mile. Inn driveway is on right.

CORNELL HOUSE

Cabaret conviviality still echoes here

A speakeasy during Prohibition, this graceful Queen Anne Victorian still echoes its colorful past.

Facing the four-hundred-acre Kennedy Park, open to the public year-round, the communal breakfast parlor with floor-to-ceiling windows is a favorite gathering spot. A deck with tables and colorful umbrellas can be glimpsed from the dining table, and guests are welcome to eat breakfast *al fresco*, when the weather permits. In the evening, dining tables transform into game tables and conversation often continues into the wee hours.

Behind the main house is Hill House, a two-story converted barn, especially charming in warm months when shuttered windows are accented with flowering window boxes. Newly developed into four luxury apartments, each unit has its own bedroom, living room, and dining room and features a private deck, galley kitchen, Jacuzzi, fireplace, and air conditioning.

Here, in a location central to both busy Lenox Center and Tanglewood, David Rolland, a former Oregon restaurateur, provides off-season weekends that include Saturday night roast duck, poached salmon, or baked scallop dinners. A ground-floor spa, with Jacuzzi, sauna, and steam room, assures total bliss.

CORNELL HOUSE. 197 Pittsfield Rd., Lenox, MA 01240; (413) 637-0562; David Rolland, host. Charming inn, circa 1888, Victorian-style. Open year-round. Nine guest rooms in main house, four luxury suites in "Hill House," all with private baths. Three night minimum in season. Rates: $330 to $375 for two people for three nights, $65 to $75 per night during week, $895 per week for suite. Off-season specials. Rates include light breakfast; excellent dining nearby. No children in main house; no pets; Visa/MasterCard. The Berkshires offer year-round recreation, cultural events, historic events, antiques.

DIRECTIONS: from New York City, take the Taconic Pkwy. to Rte. 23 exit. Take 23E through Great Barrington to Rte. 7. Take Rte. 7 to Rte. 7A (Lenox Centre) and turn left. Drive through Lenox and up hill to inn on left, just past church. From Mass. Turnpike, take Lee exit 2. Turn right onto Rte. 20W and drive through Lee. Turn left onto Rte. 183 and proceed to Lenox Centre.

HAWTHORNE INN

A stimulating haven

In the mid-1970s artist Gregory Burch was attracted to Concord and to this house, which was large enough to contain his painting and sculpture studio as well as rooms for wayfarers. He and his wife Marilyn offer guests the comforts of an impeccably maintained and antiques-filled home. Gregory's soapstone bas-relief carvings and energetic paintings, and Marilyn's beautifully designed quilts contribute, along with books of poetry and art, and Mayan and Inca artifacts, to make the Hawthorne Inn a very stimulating haven.

HAWTHORNE INN, 462 Lexington Rd., Concord, MA 01742; (508) 369-5610; Gregory Burch and Marilyn Mudry, hosts. Charming inn on site steeped in American history. Open all year. Seven guest rooms, private and shared baths. Rates: $70 single, $90 double. $20 third person. Continental breakfast. No credit cards; no pets. Wide variety of restaurants within 10-minute drive. Equally wide variety of sports and spots of interest in this scenic country.

DIRECTIONS: from Rte. 128–95, take Exit 45 west for 3½ miles. Bear right at the single blinking light. Inn is one mile on left, across from "Wayside" (Hawthorne and Alcott home).

MERRELL TAVERN INN

Fine antiques in a stagecoach inn

Catering to travelers since the 1800s, the old Merrell Tavern has been painstakingly restored to its former glory by Charles and Faith Reynolds. It is now elegantly furnished with fine Sheraton and Heppelwhite antiques the Reynolds have collected over twenty-five years. Canopied, four-poster, and pencil-post bedsteads with deluxe mattresses, sought out for their exquisite comfort, ensure a pleasurable night's sleep. In the morning guests gather in the tavern for breakfast, which may feature Charles' special omelets, pancakes, and sausages, or perhaps a new find from a cookbook. A visit will reveal more treasures; there is not space here to do them justice.

MERRELL TAVERN INN , Rte. 102, South Lee., MA 01260; (413) 243-1794; Charles and Faith Reynolds, hosts. Closed Christmas Eve and Day. Ten guest rooms, 4 with fireplaces, all with private baths. Rates: $55 to $130 double, according to season and amenities, weekend packages available. All rates include full breakfast. No pets; major credit cards; limited smoking.

DIRECTIONS: exit Mass. Turnpike at Lee (exit 2) and follow Rte. 102 three miles toward Stockbridge.

HAUS ANDREAS

Bed and breakfast with amenities

Haus Andreas, a full-service bed and breakfast, is a vacation in itself where hospitality and entertainment are the focus. Overlooking a pastoral view, the colonial mansion was built by a soldier of the American Revolution. During the summer of 1942, the estate became the residence of Queen Wilhelmina of the Netherlands and members of the royal family.

Continental breakfast is enhanced with a view that is truly inspiring—manicured lawns, birch trees, corn fields, and the mountains.

The formal, well-appointed bedrooms are clean and spare, with fussiness and embellishments kept to a minimum. Antiques in such a setting assume center spotlight.

Outdoors, volleyball, tennis, croquet, and badminton keep many guests busy; indoors, there is an exercise room. The nine-hole golf course across the street attracts many visitors, and bicycles are available to guests who want to stray a little farther.

Innkeeper Lillian Schmid's husband, Gerhard, is an internationally acclaimed chef who has cooked for the queen of England.

HAUS ANDREAS, RR 1, Box 435, Stockbridge Road, Lee, MA 01238; (413) 243-3298; Lilliane Schmid, inn-keeper. Eight guest rooms, all with private baths, three with fireplaces; suites available. Rates: seasonal rates vary greatly; summer weekends 4 nights minimum stay. A 5% charge is added to the bill for the maids. No pets; no children under ten. No out-of-state checks; Visa/MasterCard. Fine dining throughout the area.

DIRECTIONS: call for specific directions.

Left, the B & B is set in a fine old Back Bay townhouse. Above, period styles prevail in the guest rooms.

BOSTON—
TERRACE TOWNEHOUSE

A dedicated preservationist

Two blocks from Copley Place, and a short stroll from the Public Garden and Newberry Street, The Terrace Townehouse thrives under the stewardship of a dedicated and knowledgeable host. Gloria Belknap still frequents auctions, even after restoring and decorating this five-story mid-nineteenth century building in the heart of Boston. Her touch is revealed in everything—from the Victorian floral arrangements and wall-hung decorative plates, to the Brie omelets, German pancakes, and cheese blintzes she mastered in Paris while studying at La Varenne.

Four charming guest rooms offer the visitors a variety of fantasies. The Bay-windowed British Officer's Room has a half-tester bedstead and ephemera of a bygone romantic era, including walking sticks and sword, English schoolbooks, a volume of Byron's poetry, and the long white kid gloves of the woman who awaits the officer's return. The China Trade Room is awash in bright yellow, with a sea-captain's trunk, framed Chinese wedding skirt, and a panel from a Chinese wedding bed. The French Dining Room overlooks the garden.

Breakfasts are served in the privacy of the guest rooms with crystal and china. A charming backdrop for afternoon tea, the third-floor library, with its floral easy chairs and needlepoint carpet, offers books for browsing, chess, and board games.

Exhuberant Ms. Belknap enjoys sharing her beloved home and her love for the past. "To maintain an antique," she states, "is to preserve our heritage."

THE TERRACE TOWNEHOUSE, 60 Chandler St., Boston, MA 02116; (617) 350-6520; Gloria Belknap, owner. Open all year. Four guest rooms with private baths. Rates: $115 to $140 per room, including full breakfast served in room (off-season rates available). No children; no pets; no smoking; Portuguese and a little French and Spanish spoken; Visa/MasterCard.

DIRECTIONS: walking distance from Back Bay Amtrak station and 2½ blocks from Copley Place shopping mall. Local nearby landmark is I.M. Pei's Hancock Tower.

KIMBERLY GRANT PHOTOGRAPH

BOSTON—BEACON HILL

Stately guest rooms

Located on Boston's prestigious Beacon Hill and adjacent to the Massachusetts State House, the inn consists of two attached 1830s brick townhouses of twenty stately guest rooms. It is perfectly located for visiting the Boston Common, the Public Gardens, the Freedom Trail, and the Faneuil Hall/Quincy Market district.

The inn has been entirely renovated and charmingly decorated with beautiful period furnishings, and many guest rooms feature four-poster and canopied beds, decorative fireplaces, desks, private baths, and air conditioning. The rooms are striking, with floral patterns covering the walls and coordinated bed spreads and draperies complementing the tall windows that look out on the city.

An open kitchen is provided for self-serve breakfasts, and guests are always welcome to use the kitchen, the dining room, and the attractive parlors.

BEACON HILL. Attached 1830s brick townhouses with 20 guest rooms, 18 of which have private baths; there are 4 meeting rooms for conferences. Open all year. Rates: $80 single, $90 double, $15 additional guests. Includes stocked kitchen where you prepare your own full breakfast. Children welcome; no pets; no smoking; agency accepts all credit cards. Directions on reservation. *Represented by Bed and Breakfast Associates, Bay Colony Ltd., Boston, MA. (617) 449-5302.*

BOSTON—COPLEY SQUARE

A culinary treat

This restored 1863 five-story brick townhouse is set in the historic district adjacent to Boston's renowned Copley Square. It is within strolling distance of elegant restaurants, outdoor cafés, nearby theaters, the Hynes Convention Center, and bus and subway lines.

Sensitive attention to detail and gracious hospitality are the hallmark of this bed and breakfast. Each impeccable guest room offers uniquely decorative features including wide pine floors, bow windows, marble fireplaces, brass beds, armoires, full length paisley draperies, Chinese rugs, queen sized beds, and private baths. For those who would like them, four of the rooms provide a discreet galley kitchenette.

A generous full breakfast is served in the sun-filled penthouse breakfast room that is alive with skylights and views of the city. The host's culinary skills are showcased when he prepares and serves his perfectly turned blueberry buttermilk pancakes, French toast with tangy strawberry sauce, or old-fashioned scrambled eggs with succulent sausage. Those who prefer privacy are invited to enjoy a continental breakfast in their room.

COPLEY SQUARE. 1863 brick townhouse with 3 guest rooms with private baths. Open all year. Rates: $97 double, including full breakfast. Older children welcome; no pets; no smoking; agency accepts all credit cards. Directions on reservation. *Represented by Bed and Breakfast Associates, Bay Colony, Ltd., Boston, MA. (617) 449-5302.*

This guest room has a private sun porch.

BOSTON—NORTH SHORE

A family home

Set on a fourteen-acre estate, this rambling brown-shingled twenty-two room "cottage" is close to the fishing boats of Gloucester and the sailboat fleets of Manchester and scenic Rockport. There are acres of woodsy terrain to explore. It has its own tennis court, it is accessible to riding stables, and is a ten-minute walk from the beach.

Expansive and multi-leveled, the house is homey and casual. Old wood floors, comfortable plush period pieces, eyelet curtains, and large fireplaces abound. A sense of family history prevails: toys belonging to the father of the hostess, the host's father's art school diploma, over a hundred years old, passed down furniture and books, a large framed photo of the original Princeton Tiger belonging to the hostess's father (Princeton 1906).

Guests, essentially, have the run of the house.

Fires are always laid, ready to be lit, and a continental breakfast will be brought to the room upon request. A full breakfast is served near the fireplace in the ample dining room and, when weather permits, on the closed-in porch where wicker furniture overlooks the grounds.

Both guest rooms have old white iron bedsteads covered with delicate antique quilts. One room has an English charcoal grate fireplace and screened-in private deck overlooking a stand of hemlocks. The other chamber has a floral painted chest, oak desk, rag rug, and an antique white iron crib, in addition to two twin beds.

Framed on a wall a homily proclaims: "Mental health is our greatest wealth". The beauty of nature, an abiding sense of tranquility, sweet air, and the bliss of solitude here are all contributing factors.

NORTH SHORE. Twenty-two room Victorian estate on fourteen wooded acres. Open year-round. Two guest rooms each with private bath. Rates: $80 and $70 a room. Children welcome; pets welcome; no smoking; MasterCard/Visa/American Express. Close to Gloucester and Salem. Forty minutes to Boston. *Represented by Bed and Breakfast Associates, Bay Colony Ltd., Boston, MA.*

WINDAMAR HOUSE

Provincetown

In any season Windamar House is a fine place to stay. Bette Adams' Cape colonial house sits in a quiet residential pocket just "this side" of Provincetown's commercial district. Windamar has a picket-fenced front yard, gardens, a terraced backyard filled with lawn furniture, and, most importantly, a private parking lot.

Inside, the second-floor bedrooms range from a tiny cubbyhole to a room with cathedral ceiling and a wall of glass. Besides single rooms, two fully equipped apartments are available for longer stays. Original art fills all available walls throughout the house, and bedrooms are an eclectic mix of antiques and comfortable period pieces.

WINDAMAR HOUSE, 568 Commercial St., Provincetown, MA 02657; (617) 487-0599; Bette Adams, hostess. Some French spoken. Two houses joined together in the quiet east end of Provincetown. Open all year. Six guest rooms, sharing baths, and two fully equipped apartments. Rates: $50 to $80 main house, according to season and room; apartments $75 per night off season, two-night minimum, $650 per week in season; rates include continental breakfast for rooms only. Excellent dining nearby. No children; no pets; no credit cards. Provincetown offers incomparable natural setting, year-round recreation, bird-watching, whale-watching.

DIRECTIONS: Take Cape Hwy. (Rte. 6) to Provincetown. Take first exit to water and turn right on 6A. At 'V' in road bear left onto Commercial St. Windamar House is ¼ mile ahead on right. Boats and flights available from Boston.

ISAIAH HALL INN

Nestled in a quiet Cape Cod village

Mirroring the gentle and relaxed spirit of the Cape, the Isaiah B. Hall bed and breakfast is warm-spirited and homey. Innkeeper Marie Brophy has filled this rambling old home with a colorful mix of antiques, vintage quilts, stained glass, Oriental rugs, and handmade bric-a-brac. Each of the eleven guest rooms is cozy and simple, and after a good night's sleep, guests tuck into a substantial "expanded" continental breakfast of hot and cold cereals, fresh fruit, yogurt, homebaked breads, and locally-produced jams and jellies.

ISAIAH HALL B & B INN, 152 Whig Street, Dennis, MA 02638; (800) 736-0160, (508) 385-9928; Marie Brophy, host. Open mid-March to end of Oct. Eleven rooms, 10 with private baths. Rates: $50 to $90 double with extended continental breakfast. Children over 7 welcome; no pets; Visa/MasterCard/American Express accepted. Walking distance to beach, Cape playhouse, cinema, museum, village shopping, and fine restaurants. Badminton and croquet on premises. Golf and tennis nearby.

DIRECTIONS: from Rte. 6 onto Cape take exit 8 and go left 1.2 miles to Rte. 6A and right for 3.4 miles to Dennis. Past village green take left on Hope Lane to end and right on Whig to inn.

A rustic guest room in the Carriage Barn.

Innkeepers Jim and Caroline Lloýd on the porch of their bed and breakfast.

MOSTLY HALL

Cape Cod style plantation

Built in 1849 by a sea captain for his New Orleans bride, this inn is a Southern plantation-style home, perched majestically in a Cape Cod town. It received its unusual name when a visiting child walked in and marveled, "Why Mama, it's mostly hall!"

Indeed, the interior of the four-story bed and breakfast is dominated by its hallways and long, graceful staircases. The main floor features thirteen-foot ceilings and grand, full-length windows. Other architectural pleasures include a porch that wraps completely around all four sides of the inn, and a widow's walk. This cheerful, square little room, with its ten windows all around, is a favorite hideout for guests.

All of the six guest rooms occupy a corner of the inn, and feature queen-sized canopied beds. Like the spacious living room, with its Italian marble fireplace, they are elegantly decorated in a combination of antique and traditional furnishings. The home itself is set far back on a large lot, lending an air of leafy seclusion—a real treat for a Main Street inn!

There's plenty to do on Cape Cod, but one enjoyable recreation option is a small fleet of bicycles the Lloyds keep for guests.

MOSTLY HALL BED & BREAKFAST INN, 27 Main Street, Falmouth, MA 02540; (508) 548-3786; Caroline and Jim Lloyd, owners. Open mid-Feb. through New Year's. Six corner rooms with queen beds and private baths. Rates; $95 double ($20 less off season), including full gourmet breakfast. Children over 16 welcome; no pets; no smoking; German spoken; no credit cards. Day and sunset cruises from Falmouth harbor. Local summer and year-round theater.

DIRECTIONS: take Rte. 28 south to Falmouth to Main Street near village green.

THE OVER LOOK INN

A haven of British hospitality

When sea captain Barnabas Chipman built his home in 1869, he sited it on the outer reaches of Cape Cod, close enough to the Atlantic Ocean to feel a part of the sea. More than a century later, Chipman's three-story Victorian clapboard home is a bed and breakfast inn and, sitting at the edge of the Cape Cod National Seashore and close to the Audubon Wildlife Sanctuary, it offers overnight guests proximity both to the sea and to the Cape's wild but delicate natural beauty.

Besides its great location, the Over Look Inn is a haven of traditional British hospitality personified by Scottish-born innkeepers Nan and Ian Aitchison, and their sons Mark and Clive. The Aitchisons painstakingly restored this vintage sea captain's home to a gleaming finish, painting it soft butter yellow. They also diligently groom the inn's spacious lawn, which is wooded with mature

A brand new guest room.

shade trees that completely seclude it from neighbors.

The spirit of the British Isles is felt in the library, which is furnished with a leather couch and a working fireplace, because it is filled with books and memorabilia relating to Winston Churchill. And just down the hall, the Victorian billiards room seems a mandatory accoutrement to a proper British great house.

Continuing the tradition of their native island, the Aitchisons serve a full English breakfast each morning, often featuring the Scottish specialty *kedgeree*, a savory mixture of finnan haddie, rice, onions, chopped eggs, and raisins, sautéed in butter and served with a generous helping of mango chutney. At tea-time guests are supplied with traditional scones, hot and flaky and straight from the oven.

THE OVER LOOK INN, Rte. 6 (County Road), Eastham, Cape Cod, MA 02642; (508) 255-1886, (800) 356-1121; Ian and Nan Aitchison, hosts, with son Mark. Open all year. Ten rooms with private baths. Rates: $80 to $100 double, with full English breakfast. No children; no pets; Visa/MasterCard/American Express. Victorian billiard room, croquet, bicycles, library on premises. Swimming, surfing, tennis, golf, National sea shore nearby. Excellent year-round dining nearby.

DIRECTIONS: 3 miles beyond Orleans Rotary, across from Salt Pond Visitor Center of Cape Cod.

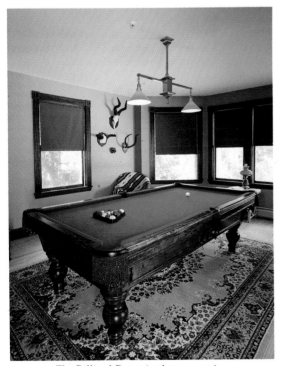

The Billiard Room in the new section.

CHARLES HINCKLEY HOUSE

Where no detail is overlooked

"A small, intimate country inn where great expectations are quietly met." The Charles Hinckley House's brochure tells the truth. The house defines elegant simplicity. Hosts Miya and Les Patrick are consummate professionals. Their goal is to indulge each guest with exquisite perfection.

Situated on the Olde Kings Highway in an historic district, the Federal Colonial house bespeaks warmth, relaxation, and romance. Every room boasts a working fireplace, private bath, and period furnishings that blend well with the rich plums and blues of the decor.

No details are overlooked. Miya's wildflower garden provides fresh bouquets to complement the exotic blooms she specially orders in. Her breakfast is a succulent testament to her aesthetic sense; choosing a combination of tropical and local fruits, she presents a platter so pleasing that it was featured in full color in *Country Living* magazine. Homemade *crème fraîche* is available

Hosts Miya and Les Patrick.

as an alternative to cream or milk, and handmade chocolates accompany the turn-down service. Flannel sheets in winter and cotton ones in summer dress the beds, with covers of down comforters or handcrafted quilts which add just the right amount of coziness. Guests also enjoy scented soaps, toiletries, thick-piled cotton bath sheets.

Evenings are casual, with impromptu gatherings in the living room; however, privacy is as easily achievable. Honeymooners can expect a bottle of champagne and breakfast in bed, if they wish.

Miya and Les, as young as they are, have been pampering people for years—first at The Inn at Phillips Mill in New Hope, Pennsylvania, then at Graywillow, also on the Cape—but never as well as they do now. A stay here will surely prove their expertise.

Very special breakfasts.

CHARLES HINCKLEY HOUSE, Box 723, Barnstable Village, MA 02630; (508) 362-9924; Les and Miya Patrick, innkeepers. Open year round. Rates: $109 to $139 with full breakfast. Four guest rooms, all with private baths and working fireplaces. Children over 12 welcome; no pets; no smoking.

DIRECTIONS: from Rte. 3 take Rte. 6 to exit 6. At the end of the ramp, turn left. Turn right onto 6A at the stop sign (½ mile down the road). Go 1½ mile more, and the house is on a slight rise to the left.

ASHLEY MANOR

Celebrating the colonial period

The warmth and elegance of the colonial period are celebrated at Ashley Manor, a bed and breakfast inn nestled in the heart of Cape Cod's historic Barnstable village. The inn is a softly weathered Cape shingle that grew, over three centuries, to become a small estate surrounded by two park-like acres. The original section of the house traces its beginnings to 1699, built when Barnstable was a tiny fishing settlement. Wide, worn floorboards gleaming with the patina of age; a massive hearth complete with beehive ovens; and a secret passage, used during the Revolutionary War, reveal the age and character of the inn's first incarnation.

Today, innkeepers Donald and Fay Bain take pride in their gracious home, and they are careful to fill it with furnishings that conform to its rich colonial atmosphere. The Bains give equal attention to providing life's graceful details, and to that end they fill rooms daily with fresh flowers; they offer guests an aperitif before dinner; and they stock bedside tables with a delightfully sinful cache of fine imported chocolates.

The inn contains six guest rooms, four of which are suites and five equipped with working fireplaces. The floorboards in several of the rooms sport original "Nantucket spackle" paint, which has been carefully preserved, and each room is decorated with fine traditional fabrics, furnishings, wallcoverings, and antiques. The end result is thoroughly elegant and romantic.

Come the morning, guests find Donald hard at work in the kitchen preparing their morning feast. During summer months, breakfast at Ashley Manor is served *al fresco* on a brick terrace overlooking the inn's well-groomed grounds and new, private tennis court. When cool weather sets in, guests gather in the lovely old dining room. Here they relax in front of a blazing hearth and admire the Bains' collection of fine antique china.

ASHLEY MANOR, P.O. Box 856, 3660 Old Kings Highway (Rte. 6A), Barnstable, MA 02630; (508) 362-8044; Donald and Fay Bain, hosts. Open all year. Six rooms with private baths. Rates: $100 to $165, with full, multi course gourmet breakfast. Children over 14 welcome; no pets; Visa/MasterCard/American Express; French spoken. Croquet played on premises; bicycles available. Swimming, tennis, golf, antiquing, arts and crafts, other Cape Cod activities.

DIRECTIONS: take Rte. 6A East through village of Barnstable to light. Go straight through light for 9/10 miles to manor on left.

The Olmsted Suite has two bedrooms and a sun deck.

Innkeepers Sal DiFlorio and Brian Gallo.

THE INN AT FERNBROOK

Gardens by Olmsted

This inn is a glorious reminder of what truly were "the good old days"—when summer homes were mansions, and gardens were replicas of Eden. In 1881, a Boston restaurateur built this sprawling Queen Anne Victorian and hired the famous landscape architect, Frederick Law Olmsted, to do the gardens on the surrounding seventeen acres. Olmsted, who designed New York's Central Park, created a magnificent retreat.

The inn itself is luxuriously decorated with Victorian furniture, but in a light, airy style. Rooms are flooded with sunshine through sheer curtains, and Oriental rugs complement softly-printed wallpapers in shades of cream-white. Each of the six guest rooms is very private, thanks to a design that has no two bedrooms sharing a common wall.

Honeymooners will particularly love staying in the Garden Cottage, a guest accommodation behind the main house, complete with the proverbial white picket fence. Also delightful is the third-floor suite.

A loft overlooks its living room, and it has its own sun deck with views of the gardens.

Though commercialism has claimed most of the Cape, guests will not feel its influence in Centerville, an 'un-touristy' town. Owners Brian Gallo and Sal DiFlorio have wonderful suggestions for visits to workshops of Cap Cod artisans. Brian can steer you to small shops and galleries offering everything from folk art to collectible glassware and colonial furniture. Sal is trained in European bodywork, and is available, by appointment, for relaxing therapeutic massage. Breakfast is four full courses, served in the dining room or on the porch.

You will be pleased to learn that, as a guest here, you are in good company. Those preceding you include Hollywood greats Cecil B. DeMille and Walt Disney, as well as Presidents Kennedy and Nixon!

THE INN AT FERNBROOK, 481 Main Street, Centerville, MA 02632; (508) 775-4334; Fax (508) 778-4455; Brian Gallo and Sal DiFlorio, owners. Open all year. Six guest rooms and a private one-room cottage, all with private baths; suite with private living room available. Rates: $105 to $185 double ($20 less off season), including full, 4-course breakfast. Children over 13 welcome; no pets; smoking in parlor or on porch only; Italian, Spanish, German spoken; all credit cards accepted. Wide range of dining nearby, including a Northern Italian cuisine restaurant that will pick up guests at the inn. All the usual Cape Cod activities.

DIRECTIONS: on the main street of Centerville, on Cape Cod off Rte. 6, exit 5.

DAVE MONAGHAN PHOTOGRAPHS

CLIFF LODGE

Sample the romance of island living

Once the province of whaling barons, who built stately mansions on cobblestone streets, Nantucket is now an elite summer retreat of cedar-shake beach houses, gourmet restaurants, boutiques, and bed and breakfasts: To sample the old days there is the Nantucket Whaling Museum, where the island's history is celebrated.

Pretty enough to have graced the cover of *Country Home* magazine, Cliff Lodge belies its 1771 birthdate. Previously run as Harbor House, and just five minutes from the center of town, it was given a facelift by two women from Nantucket Island Antiques. Using soft blues and whites, Laura Ashley wallpapers and fabrics, and framed pastoral prints, they created a light cheerful feeling in the eleven guest rooms, six of which have ocean views. Sprightly in décor, the entire house is furnished with bright wicker, antique pine pieces, and spatter-painted floors.

A second-floor alcove, with its wicker chairs and writing table, is perfect for relaxation, as is the second-floor porch that overlooks the harbor and Jetty's Beach. For those who dote on a panoramic view, there are steps leading up to the widow's walk, where the view spans the entire island.

Breakfast includes delicious homemade muffins or fruit breads which can be eaten in front of the fireplace in the breakfast room.

In 1990, the national newspaper *USA Today* included Cliff Lodge as one of the ten most romantic inns in the country. Need we say more?

CLIFF LODGE, 9 Cliff Road, Nantucket, MA 02554; (508) 228-9480; Gerri Miller, manager. Open all year. Eleven rooms and full apartment with private entrance, all with private baths, TVs, telephones. Rates: $35 to $60 single, $50 to $150 double, $105 to $190 for apartment, varying with seasons. Includes ample continental breakfast plus afternoon tea in season. Children 10 and over welcome; no pets; smoking allowed; Visa/MasterCard/American Express. Parking on premises. Overlooks beach and harbor.

DIRECTIONS: 7 minutes from ferry, 5 minutes from downtown.

The Capt. Harding Room has a fireplace and a bay window.

CAPTAIN DEXTER HOUSE

Island living at its best

Three blocks from the ferry, and the first home in the historic residential district of Vineyard Haven, The Captain Dexter House stands as a model of elegance, comfort, and convenience. Guests here can experience island living at its best—without billboards, fast-food franchises, not even stoplights—only picturesque seaside villages, quiet harbors, and glorious white sand beaches.

Martha's Vineyard is world-renowned for its natural beauty as well as its celebrities. The flat, straight southern shore provides miles of glacially carved, wave-dashed beach. The gentle curves on the island's other two sides lead into the calmer waters of Nantucket Sound to the east and Vineyard Sound to the west. North and center lies the year-round town.

The innkeeper likes to describe the old sea captain's house as a "Federalized Victorian" with a peaked roof, bay windows, and side porch, but the interior recalls colonial times. A Williamsburg-style reproduction table assumes center stage in the dining room, flanked by Queen Anne-style chairs and beyond by a Sheraton breakfront and a Scottish grandfather clock that dates back to 1812. The far wall hosts two portraits painted in 1843, the same year that the house was built.

The eight well-kept guest rooms reflect the consideration put into the common rooms. Antiques and contemporary furnishings provide a pleasing mix that suits modern demands for comfort and charm.

THE CAPTAIN DEXTER HOUSE, Box 2457, 100 Main Street, Vineyard Haven, Martha's Vineyard, MA 02568; (508) 693-6564; Roberta Pieczenik, owner. Open all year. Eight guest rooms, all with private baths, two with working fireplaces. Rates: $100 to $165 in season; $65 to $175 off-season; $15 for an additional person. Children over sixteen are welcome; no pets; smoking in guest rooms only; MasterCard/Visa/American Express. Continental breakfast. Guest refrigerator, beach towels, locked garage for bicycles. Watersports; horseback riding; summer theater; good restaurants nearby.

DIRECTIONS: Car reservations to and from Woods Hole should be made well in advance. Write or call the Parkers.

RHODE ISLAND

ADMIRAL FITZROY INN

An inn to lift your spirits

An immaculate three-story, weathered-shingle hotel, the Admiral Fitzroy, one of the most enjoyable inns in Newport, is the brainchild of owner Jane Berriman and her husband Bruce. It is just one of three sister inns—the others being the Admiral Benbow and the Admiral Farragut—operated by the Berrimans, and each has its own character and style. The Berrimans are seasoned travelers who bring to innkeeping a refined sense of what the road-weary relish. At the Admiral Fitzroy this means all the amenities of an intimate, fine hotel with an abundance of grace notes usually reserved for home-style bed and breakfast inns.

The Admiral Fitzroy is tucked well away from the busy thoroughfare of Thames Street, but it offers wonderful views of the harbor and is perfectly located for walking the town. The inn is artfully conceived and is a showcase for fine craftsmanship, from the hand-carved Admiral Fitzroy plaque in the lobby (which was created by Bruce, a master woodcarver) to the hand painted, lacquered, and glazed wall treatments that add luster and richness to each room. Beds are dressed in fine linens, topped by plush down comforters. The innkeepers also attend to such welcome details as using fresh herbs in the breakfast omelet and offering guests fresh mint to flavor their coffee and tea.

The quality of service at the Admiral Fitzroy is top-notch. The inn's fine staff is congenial and one and all take great pride in working for this special inn.

ADMIRAL FITZROY INN, 398 Thames Street, Newport, RI 02840; (401) 846-4256; Jane Berriman, proprietor; Brenda Johnston, host. Open Feb. 1 to Jan. 5. Eighteen rooms with private baths. Rates: winter $80 to $105; summer $125 to $145 with full breakfast. Children welcome; no pets; Visa/MasterCard/American Express. Newport activities, including sailing, swimming, golf. Extensive dining opportunities.

DIRECTIONS: located in downtown Newport, on the main street facing the harbor.

A top-floor bedroom, with balcony, overlooks Newport harbor.

WAYSIDE GUEST HOUSE

On the Street of Dreams

This 1896 Newport "Summer Cottage" is across from The Elms and down the block from Belcourt Castle, Mrs. Astor's Beechwood, and the venerable Rosecliff, where *The Great Gatsby* was filmed.

Everything in the interior is generously proportioned with fifteen-foot ceilings on the parlor floor, and twelve-foot ceilings in the guest rooms. The nine bedchambers are elegantly ample, and each has a large sitting area where breakfast may be enjoyed in the privacy of the room. All of the rooms are furnished with turn-of-the-century furniture, and five of the rooms have beautifully detailed decorative fireplaces. All have private baths.

Outdoors there is a heated in-ground swimming pool, provided with deck chairs and chaises, and surrounded by poplars and beech trees. A barbecue and picnic tables are available for those who choose to eat on the grounds.

Great restaurants are easy to find, and the Posts recommend White Horse Tavern, The Black Pearl, and La Petite Auberge for formal dining. Try The Canfield House or The Moorings for casual fare.

Dorothy Post dreamed of having a bed and breakfast when she was in high school and wrote of it in her senior yearbook. In 1976 she and her husband Al bought the Wayside, which once served as a girls' dorm for Newport College. After fifteen years of owning and managing the Wayside with their son Don and daughter-in-law Debbie, Dorothy is glad her day dream came true.

WAYSIDE GUEST HOUSE, 406 Bellevue Avenue, Newport, RI 02840; (401) 847-0302; Dorothy, Al, Don, and Debbie Post, owners and managers. Open all year. Nine guest rooms with private baths. Rates: $95 to $105 double, including continental breakfast. Children welcome; no pets; smoking allowed; no credit cards. The dining and other recreational activities in Newport are legendary.

DIRECTIONS: on famous Bellevue Ave. across the street from The Elms.

Lifestyle in the Grand Manner.

CLIFFSIDE INN

The grandeur of the Victorian age

Cliffside Inn captures the grandeur of the Victorian age with flowing curtains, bay windows, and commodious common rooms. This Second Empire summer cottage, which now stands among many beautiful houses in a peaceful residential district, once dominated the acreage. But even as times have changed, the luxury of the inn remains, as exemplified by the hallway floor's coat of arms, the last remnant of Cliffside's grand ballroom which burned down decades ago.

The eleven guest rooms, all with private bath facilities, are imaginatively decorated. The coral and dark sea green of Miss Adele's Room is incorporated into a fireplace mantel that now functions as a headboard for the queen-sized bed. The Miss Beatrice Room, a favorite with newlyweds, is dressed in pinks and blues with bay windows and a Lincoln bed. Repeat visitors often ask for the light-filled Arbor Room situated off the porch. Its glass wall reminded one visitor of being in a botanical conservatory.

Cliffside has an unusual history. Built in 1880, the house served as a summer retreat for the governor of Maryland. Sixteen years later it became the site of a private preparatory school. The most famous denizen was Beatrice Pastorius Turner, who gained fame as a self-portrait artist and who painted the mother-daughter oil painting that hangs in the living room on the wall to the right of the piano. Her notoriety, however, came from her eccentricities. A recluse obsessed with youth, she walked into the town wearing Victorian clothes up until the 1940s.

Cliff Walk is about a ten-minute stroll away; the beach, even closer. All in all, Cliffside is a welcome addition to Newport's attractions.

CLIFFSIDE INN, 2 Seaview Avenue, Newport, RI 02840; (401) 847-1811; Annette King, innkeeper. Open all year. Eleven guest rooms, all with private baths. Rates: $115 to $185. The rate includes tax and a full breakfast and evening hors d'oeuvres. Children over 13 welcome; no pets.

DIRECTIONS: from I-95, take Rte. 138 over the Newport Bridge. Take a right onto Americas Cup Ave. and bear left onto Memorial Blvd. Take a right onto Cliff Ave. The inn is on the left, at the corner of Sea View Ave.

JAILHOUSE INN

A 1772 jail

If the urge to escape the daily grind causes guilt that borders on the criminal, Newport's Jail House Inn is the perfect destination for a quick getaway. The inn is thoroughly acquainted with offenders of every stripe, having served as Newport's house of detention since it was built in 1772. When the police moved their headquarters in 1985, Newport developer Don Glassie bought the property and converted the rambling edifice into a unique bed and breakfast inn.

Guest accommodations range from rooms in the "cell block" and "maximum security" to "solitary confinement." Each is comfortably furnished with sturdy, denim-upholstered furniture, which fits right in with the institutional grey carpeting and stark white walls. The inn deviates from the penal theme by equipping each bedroom with a television and telephone.

JAILHOUSE INN, 13 Marlborough Street, Newport, RI 02840; (401) 847-4638; Don Glassie, owner; Katie De Costa, manager. Open all year. Twenty-two rooms with private baths. Rates: seasonal, varying from $55 to $125 double, $5 for extra person. Children welcome; no pets; Visa/MasterCard/American Express accepted. Viewing the Newport mansions a must, plus swimming, tennis, boating, and eating seafood.

DIRECTIONS: from "Scenic Newport" exit turn right to second light and right again to light where fire station is on left. Turn left—inn is 2 blocks up on right. From Boston on Rte. 114 bear right at fork in road after police station and turn right onto Marlborough Street.

BRINLEY VICTORIAN INN

Unpretentious, well-tended

On a quiet street off the beaten track, yet close to both the bustle of town and the mansions of Bellevue Avenue, the Brinley Victorian Inn is really two houses, a mansard-roofed Victorian frame and a smaller, adjoining counterpart. The parlor in the main house is formal and eye-pleasing, filled with Victorian settees, a rocker, and lace-draped tables, all in soft shades of green and cream. In the evening, guests congregate here, or in the game room at the rear of the house, comparing notes on the day's activities, preparing the next day's schedule, or relaxing over a game of cards. The overall atmosphere at the Brinley is unpretentious, friendly, well-tended, and relaxed.

THE BRINLEY VICTORIAN INN, 23 Brinley St., Newport, RI 02840; (401) 849-7645; Peter Carlisle, host; Dr. Edwina Sebest and Amy Weintraub, owners. Open year-round; Seventeen guest rooms; thirteen with private baths and air conditioning. Two newly restored Victorian houses connected by walkway. Rates by room: winter, $55 to $90, summer, $85 to $130; $15 per extra person in room. Continental breakfast. No children under twelve; no pets; checks accepted. Extensive dining in area.

DIRECTIONS: from Newport/Jamestown bridge (Rte. 138), take downtown Newport exit. Go to third light and turn left onto Touro. At second light, turn left on Kay, and then right on Brinley. From north, take Rte. 114 into downtown. At movie theaters, bear left onto Touro and repeat above directions.

Pampered luxury typical of Newport living.

FRANCIS MALBONE HOUSE

A shipping merchant's mansion

Attributed to Peter Harrison, architect of the Touro Synagogue and the Redwood Library, this historic inn was built in 1760 for Colonel Francis Malbone. Having made his fortune as a shipping merchant, Malbone moored his fleet in Newport Harbor across from his mansion. Legend has it that there was once an underground tunnel from the waterfront to the mansion through which the colonel smuggled goods to avoid paying duty to King George.

Painstakingly maintained throughout the years, and a private residence until 1989, the mansion has eight guest rooms and one suite. Furnished in the Queen Anne style, with wide floor boards and four poster beds, some of the rooms have working fireplaces, and each is painted in either terra cotta, dresden blue, hunter green, or burgundy.

Two sitting rooms on the first floor face the harbor, one room still paneled in the original 1760 carved wood. Both have inside shutters. A third sitting room houses the library.

Breakfast is served in the dining room, originally the mansion's kitchen, with its open walk-in hearth. Freshly baked muffins and croissants, yogurt, and occasionally apple crisp are served.

A large terrace in the walled-in garden is perfect for dining outdoors, where a flowering dogwood tree towers over the fountain. A paper bark maple, a copper beech, dahlias, and rhododendron all add to the lovely, serene ambience of this colonial mansion in the heart of the waterfront district.

THE FRANCIS MALBONE HOUSE, 392 Thames Street, Newport, RI 02840; (401) 846-0392; Jim Maher, innkeeper. Open all year. Eight guest rooms and 1 suite, all with private baths. Rates: $125 to $225 in season (May 1 to Oct. 31); $80 to $125 off season (all rates per room). Includes continental breakfast. Children over 12 welcome; no pets; no smoking; French spoken; Visa/MasterCard/American Express. Recommended restaurants include The Chart House, Le Bistro, The Black Pearl. The fabulous attractions of Newport include the Tennis Hall of Fame, Touro Synagogue, Redwood Library, international music festivals, world-class tennis and yachting.

DIRECTIONS: located downtown on the harborfront. For guest parking take third left off Thames onto Brewer St.

CONNECTICUT

JOHN KANE PHOTOGRAPHS

THE HOUSE ON THE HILL

Architectural gem

A legacy of Waterbury's heyday, when it was renowned for its brass and clockworks, this Stick-style Queen Anne Victorian was built by Wallace Camp, the inventor of the post office box. Along with other architectural gems, it remains to be admired long after Waterbury's era of wealthy mill-owners who erected them has vanished.

Built over a hundred years ago, the house on the hill has been lovingly restored by owner Marianne Vandenburgh. Original cherry, oak, and mahogany floors, fireplaces, and built-ins provide a backdrop that imbues the interior with richness and warmth. The deep rust walls in the parlor, with its velvet, paisley, and crewel work, combine with vintage

Left, top, the richly carved woodwork of the striking sitting room; bottom, an utterly charming guest room.

bound books, artfully assembled dried flowers, and lyrical sculpture to create the overwhelmingly romantic mood of *Victoria Magazine*.

The lace-filled breakfast room, with its down-pillowed wicker settees, is the setting for the corn-meal pancakes and homemade berry sauce that guests adore. Afternoon tea or sherry is served with homemade sweets.

The house affords the multi-talented Ms. Vandenburgh the opportunity to display her decorating, hosting, and culinary gifts. Even her acting ability has been tapped. When Jane Fonda rented the house during the filming of *Stanley & Iris*, Ms. Vandenburgh appeared in one of the scenes.

THE HOUSE ON THE HILL, 92 Woodlawn Terrace, Waterbury, CT 06710; (203) 757-9901; Marianne Vandenburgh, owner. Open all year. Five guest rooms, 4 with private baths, 1 sharing. Rates: $65 to $100 per room, including breakfast. No pets; no smoking; no credit cards; a little Spanish spoken. Good restaurants on Waterbury green. Family recreation on Lake Quassapaug.

DIRECTIONS: from I-84 to Waterbury take exit 21 and go right on Meadow St. (which becomes Willow) to Pine. Take right up hill past Woodlawn Terrace to first driveway on left, up to house.

RED BROOK INN

A colonial gem near Mystic Seaport

Sitting in a California Victorian house filled with a lifetime's collection of Early American antiques, Ruth Keyes came to the conclusion that she would never feel altogether at home in the West. An old fashioned girl at heart, she dreamt of Connecticut and a colonial village like Old Mystic. Within six months of her return to the East, she owned the beautiful 1770 Creary Homestead.

A recent and welcome addition expanding the inn is The Historic Haley Tavern, originally a stage coach stop. Restored and beautifully appointed, its rooms include The Ross Haley Chamber with antique furnishings and working fireplace, The Mary Virginia Chamber, a beautiful Early American room with a canopied queen bed, and The Victorian Nancy Creary Chamber with its own whirlpool tub.

Under Ruth's guardianship, the Red Brook Inn is a colonial showcase. Her collection of furniture and artifacts perfectly complements both the lines and the spirit of the house. All of the rooms are filled with period antiques, from the second-floor bedrooms with their blanket chests and early lighting devices, to the first-floor keeping room with its original cooking fireplace, beehive oven, and iron crane and cookware. Each four-poster or canopied bed is coordinated with carefully chosen matching quilts and linens.

A full breakfast, served on the long harvest table in the keeping room, might include quiche, baked or fresh fruit, eggs Benedict, walnut waffles, or berry pancakes.

THE RED BROOK INN, Box 237, Rte. 184 at Wells Rd., Old Mystic, CT 06372; (203) 572-0349; Ruth Keyes, proprietor and host. Colonial gem built around 1770. Historic Haley Tavern circa 1740. Open year-round. Eleven guest rooms; all with private baths, eight with working fireplaces. Rates: $90–$170 per double room, including a full breakfast. No pets; no smoking in building; Visa/MasterCard. Mystic Seaport Museum, Mystic Aquarium, horseback riding, golf, sailing, submarine tour cruises on river, Coast Guard Academy nearby. Excellent dining in area.

DIRECTIONS: take I-95 to exit 89 (Allyn St.); go north 1½ miles to light (Rte. 184 Gold Star Hwy.), Turn right and go east ⅕ mile. Inn is on left, up the hill.

INN AT CHAPEL WEST

New Haven extravaganza

Originally slated to become posh new office space, this eighteenth-century mansion has blossomed into a bed and breakfast on the revitalized upper Chapel Street. Once an unofficial Yale fraternity house, it is a fresh bouquet to the neighborhood and a symbol of New Haven's commitment to the restoration and reclamation of its heritage.

Eclectic in its décor, the guest rooms have faux marble door panels hinting at color schemes within. Room 34 has a cloudscape painted by Connecticut muralist Peter Perry, a brass bedstead, a pine hope chest, and soft lavender, pink, and blue appointments. Room 21 has a lace-draped day bed and Austrian shades, while Room 11 has Laura Ashley fabrics, a pressed tin ceiling, a velvet paisley chair, and Victorian face masks. All of the beds, piled high with cushions and goose-down pillows, are bedecked with ruffles and look wonderfully inviting. Some of the rooms have gas-lit fireplaces, and all of them have

Room 23, with poppy-colored walls and a working fireplace.

comfortable chairs, writing desks, telephones, and televisions. Bathrooms have pedestal sinks, blow dryers, and shower radios.

Continental breakfast, buffet-style, is served in the dining room and a catered dinner can be arranged. A tour of Yale, theater tickets to one of New Haven's many musical or dramatic offerings, transportation, and secretarial or babysitting services are happily attended to. The India Palace, Miya's, and Hot Tomatos, serving Indian, Japanese, and Italian food respectively, are literally a stone's throw away.

In addition to housing visitors to Yale and people on business, the inn has already had its share of celebrities. Chuck Norris slept here, as did the moms of Cybil Shepard and Sylvester Stallone.

THE INN AT CHAPEL WEST, 1201 Chapel Street, New Haven, CT 06511; (203) 777-1201; fax: (203) 776-7363; Steven Schneider, host. Open all year. Ten guest rooms, all with private baths, telephone, color TV; some with fireplaces. Rates: $125 to $175, including continental breakfast. Children welcome; no pets; smoking allowed; all major credit cards. Handicap accessible. The inn is less than four blocks from Yale's Old Campus, New Haven Green, and minutes from New Haven's 30 plus pizza places.

DIRECTIONS: inn is located on Chapel Street, the main shopping street of downtown New Haven, leading to the green. Call for directions.

Room 33, with superb antique Victorian pieces.

The Jenny Lind Room.

BISHOP'S GATE INN

Theater people

Bishop's Gate Inn, located in the center of town, is a gem. Established by Julie Bishop, who worked with the Goodspeed actors, the theatrical tradition is being carried on by current innkeepers Molly and Dan Swartz.

Besides the full breakfast, which might include stuffed French toast, buttermilk pancakes, or hearty egg dishes, the innkeepers offer guests dinner if they request it in advance.

Each bedroom is completely comfortable and most display handsome early American furnishings and accessories. The Director's Suite is dramatic with its beamed cathedral ceiling, private balcony, and "Hollywood" bathroom complete with double sinks, sauna, and sitting area.

BISHOP'S GATE INN, Goodspeed Landing, East Haddam, CT 06423; (203) 873-1677; Dan and Molly Swartz, hosts. Colonial built in 1818 and filled with family antiques. Six guest rooms, all with private baths. Open year-round: $75–100 double. No children under six, no pets; Visa/MasterCard/Discover, checks accepted. Hearty full breakfast; picnic lunches can be arranged. Many wonderful restaurants a short drive away. Goodspeed Opera House, museums, state parks, Connecticut River cruises, airstrip on riverbank.

DIRECTIONS: from New York City, Providence, or Boston, take Connecticut Tnpke. (I-95) to exit 69 to Rte. 9. From Rte. 9, take exit 7 to East Haddam. Cross bridge and go straight on Rte. 82 for 1 block. Inn driveway is on left.

THE PALMER INN

Mansion by-the-sea

Skillfully crafted by his shipbuilders, this turn-of-the-century eighteen-room seaside mansion was constructed for Robert Palmer, Jr., an owner of the largest wooden shipbuilding company on the East Coast in its day. Today the house carries on as an elegant inn.

Tastefully furnished with Victorian furniture, period wallpapers, brass fixtures, and antique appointments, the inn boasts a good measure of family heirlooms. Original and unusual stained-glass windows add drama to the rooms, and lush flowers and herb gardens adorn the spacious grounds.

THE PALMER INN, 25 Church Street, Noank, CT 06340; (203) 572-9000; Patricia White Cornish, host. Open year round. Six spacious guest rooms with private baths. Rates: $105 to $175; includes pleasant continental breakfast. Children sixteen and over; no pets; no smoking in guest rooms or dining area; Visa/MasterCard. Dachshunds on premises. Within walking distance of tennis, sailing, art galleries, swimming, and fine lobster house.

DIRECTIONS: take I-95 to exit 89, Allyn Street. From north take a right (and from south a left) and travel through two traffic lights across Rte. 1 onto West Mystic Avenue to stop sign. Turn right onto Noank Road (Route 215) and travel 1.7 miles to stop sign. Turn left onto Mosher, past fire house, and turn left onto Main Street. Go 1 block and left onto Church. Tall hedges surround inn. Guest parking in back of inn.

A seaside mansion crafted by shipwrights.

This public room, used for breakfast, is disarmingly colonial.

RIVERWIND INN

Collections everywhere

Riverwind, a delightful country inn, is nestled on Main Street in the Connecticut River Valley town of Deep River. Native Virginian Barbara Barlow has turned the rambling colonial-era home into a wonderful blend of New England charm and down-home Southern hospitality.

The décor is colonial, with an eclectic folksy touch. Featured are an extraordinary antique quilt collection, farm and cooking implements, dried herbs and flowers, hand-stencilled walls, and one-of-a-kind furniture, much of it from Barbara's family.

Eight guest rooms are charmingly appointed. The Havlow Room has an early pine bed with hand-painted rose panels on the headboard and an exquisitely embroidered "crazy" quilt. Zelda's Suite, a two-room Gatsby-era hideaway, and the Champagne and Roses Room are particularly romantic.

Barbara and her husband, Bob Bucknall, like to describe their place as "anti-formal." With eight common areas throughout the inn, guests can either mingle or find a special place to be alone.

There are collections of collections everywhere, from old playbills to handmade dolls. Pigs play prominently in the décor, owing to Barbara's childhood in Smithfield ham country. And the country breakfast always includes pig-shaped biscuits.

RIVERWIND INN, 209 Main Street, Deep River, CT 06417; (203) 526-2014; Barbara Barlow and Bob Bucknall, owners. Open all year. Eight guest rooms with private baths and air conditioning; one with 2 queens, one suite with double and twin beds. Rates: $85 to $145 per room, including full country breakfast. Children over 12 welcome; no pets; smoking allowed; small surcharge on credit cards. Famous Goodspeed Opera House, Essex steam train, riverboat cruises nearby.

DIRECTIONS: enquire when making reservations.

Innkeepers Bob Bucknall and Barbara Barlow.

WEST LANE INN

Sample the good life in a private mansion

A New England getaway close to city bustle, the West Lane Inn in historic Ridgefield, Connecticut, is just fifty miles from New York City. This bed and breakfast inn contains more rooms than most, so guests don't always share their morning muffin and coffee with owner Maureen Mayer. But they enjoy the solid comforts evident throughout this grand, early nineteenth-century mansion. Among the amenities generally found only in fine hotels

are thick padded carpets and a double thickness of door between adjoining rooms, which helps maintain the prevailing sense of quiet and privacy. Bathrooms are equipped with heated towel racks, full-length mirrors, and, in some cases, bidets. An adjoining house, called the Cottage, contains suites with service kitchens and private decks that open onto a vast expanse of well-manicured lawn. A simple room service menu, an optional full breakfast, king and queen-size beds, a tennis court, and one-day laundry and dry cleaning service make the West Lane Inn a welcome haven for tired wayfarers and business travelers.

WEST LANE INN, 22 West Lane, Ridgefield, CT 06877; (203) 438-7323; Maureen Mayer, hostess. Former private mansion invites guests to sample the good life. Open all year. Fourteen guest rooms in main house, two with working fireplaces; six suites in rear cottage, all with private baths. Rates: $90 single, $110 double, including continental breakfast; full breakfast available for extra charge. Good dining in area. Children welcome, cribs and playpens available; no pets; major credit cards; no checks. Ridgefield offers Revolutionary War sites, tours, museums; cross-country and downhill skiing.

DIRECTIONS: from NYC, take the FDR to the Major Deegan to Saw Mill Pkwy. Stay on Saw Mill to end and exit onto Rte. 35 going east. Drive approximately 12 miles to Ridgefield. Inn is on Rte. 35.

A portrait of the son of the original owner hangs in the stairwell.

BUTTERNUT FARM

An impressive, small museum

Butternut Farm in Glastonbury, Connecticut, is an especially fine example of pre-Revolutionary architecture. The oldest section of the house was built by Jonathan Hale in 1720, a well-to-do gentleman with an eye for fine moldings and a feel for proportion—rare commodities in early homes. By the mid-1700s, a keeping room, "borning room," buttery, and extra bedchambers were added as Hale's family grew.

Present owner Don Reid is a faithful steward to this architectural gem. He loves early American antiques and has collected many excellent examples from the period, including an antique pencil post canopied bed, an exquisite cherry highboy, and pre-Revolutionary bottles and Bennington pottery marbles.

The keeping room has beams bedecked with drying herbs and flowers. An antique settle and variety of chairs surround the large hearth, whose magnitude is completely overshadowed by the second fireplace found in the adjoining dining room. This brick hearth, of mammoth proportions, is teamed up with an oversized antique dining table and bannister-back chairs. An oil painting of Jonathan Hale's son is prominently displayed.

Guest rooms upstairs are decorated with wing-back chairs, wooden chests, and antique hat-boxes. Museum quality, hand-hooked rugs brighten softly gleaming, wide-plank pine floorboards.

Continuously occupied since its construction, the house shares its charm with appreciative guests. A carefully tended museum of Americana, this inn is like another world—one that should be visited and revisited to enjoy its many facets.

BUTTERNUT FARM , 1654 Main St., Glastonbury, CT 06033; (203) 633-7197; Don Reid, host. Elegant house built in 1720, with a wealth of interesting architectural detail. Open year-round. Two guest rooms, shared baths; two apartments with private baths. Rates: $65 single, $65 to $83 double. Full breakfast. Checks and Visa/MasterCard/American Express accepted; no pets; smoking discouraged. Good dining in town and in adjoining Hartford.

DIRECTIONS: take I-84 or I-91 to Rte. 2 exit. Follow Rte. 2 and take exit 8; go right toward Glastonbury Center. Drive to Main St. and turn left. Drive 1.6 miles, and inn is on left. Enter from Whapley Road.

In the English country style.

MANOR HOUSE

One of Connecticut's finest

A beautiful turn-of-the-century mansion, the Manor House in Norfolk, Connecticut, with wood-paneled walls and huge stone fireplaces, is the setting for a bed and breakfast inn *par excellence.*

The innkeepers, who love classical music, have formed a novel partnership with neighbors Carl and Marilee Dudash, who make beautifully decorated harpsichords the purchase of which entitles you to a free stay at the inn.

Horse-drawn sleigh and carriage rides are provided for guests during the appropriate season after breakfasts of fresh farm eggs, bacon, orange waffles, blueberry pancakes, French toast, homemade breads, muffins, and coffee.

The 18-room house was built in 1898 by Charles Spofford, designer of London's Underground and son of Ainsworth Rand Spofford, head of the Library of Congress under President Lincoln. The interior is distinctly Victorian, with elegantly carved furniture, ornate fixtures, leaded-glass windows, and billowy white curtains.

MANOR HOUSE. P.O. Box 447, Maple Avenue, Norfolk, CT 06058; (203) 542-5690; Diane and Henry Tremblay, hosts. Open all year. Nine guest rooms, 7 with private baths, some with fireplaces and private balconies. Rates: $60-$75 single, $65-$130 double; includes full breakfast. Children over 12 welcome; no pets (boarding kennels nearby). Yale Summer School of Music and Art an annual event in Norfolk; crafts, antiques, theater, golf, swimming, and skiing.

DIRECTIONS: take I-84 to exit for Rte. 8 north at Waterbury, Conn. Go north to end of Rte. 8 at Winsted and take Rte. 44 west to Norfolk and Maple Avenue. From Massachusetts take Turnpike west to Rte. 7 exit and go south to Canaan and east on Rte. 44 to Norfolk.

GREENWOODS GATE

Exquisitely inviting

Summer visitors to the Norfolk Chamber Music Festival may have discovered Greenwoods Gate. If not, they are in for a treat. This beautiful clapboard-and-shuttered colonial house bursts forth with equal chords of romantic ambience, exquisite furnishings, and tasty dining.

Deanne Raymond and daughter Marianne have filled the house with all manner of luxuries to stimulate the senses. The spacious Darius Phelps Room, in muted tones of peach and green, has upholstered peach headboards, matching comforters, and a perfume-laden Victorian dressing table. Adjoining is a bath with a six-foot ball-and-claw-footed tub.

Separate from the rest of the house, the Levi Thompson Suite, on two levels, has rich native cherrywood, soft pastels, and a luxurious spa with steam enclosure and whirlpool. Covered in Ralph Lauren wall covering and fabrics, the E.J. Trescott Suite, in Delft blue and white, has a luxurious brass-and-iron bed, a handsome Empire chest, and a delightfully furnished four-story doll's house perched atop a blanket chest.

Breakfast is festive, starting with orange juice blended into a froth, and a choice of hearty fare served on Limoges china. Old-fashioned Irish oatmeal, a cold-weather staple, is followed by such entrées as apple-puff pancakes with hot maple syrup, triple-cheese spinach omelets, or bananas sautéed in apricot or orange marmalade flavored with triple sec and served with yogurt. All are prepared in the tin-ceilinged kitchen, including the paper-doll or heart-shaped pancakes for the younger set.

An inviting country setting.

Where sweet dreams are assured.

GREENWOODS GATE, 105 Greenwood Road East, Norfolk, CT 06058; (203) 542-5439; Deanne Raymond, owner. Open all year except Christmas Eve and Christmas Day. Three guest suites with private baths. Rates: $135 to $185 per room high season; $120 to $150 off season. Includes full gourmet breakfast. Children 12 and over welcome; no pets but kennel nearby; no smoking; Visa/MasterCard/American Express. Yale School of Music summer concerts in Norfolk; Tanglewood nearby. Winter cross-country skiing, summer golf and tennis.

DIRECTIONS: on Rte. 44 east of Norfolk village green ½ mile. Call for more details.

NEW YORK

DAVE MONAGHAN PHOTOGRAPH

PLUM BUSH

A jewel

Surrounded by a grove of towering maple trees and bedecked in mauve and pale pink with soft green and teal trim, Plumbush has been thoughtfully restored to its former Victorian elegance. Sandy Green first noticed the house as she rode to school on the bus. After growing up and moving out West, she and her husband George have returned to Chautauqua County and established a jewel of a bed and breakfast.

Each of the four bedchambers is named after a species of plum: Pipestone, the largest of the rooms; Bluefre, bedecked in blues and pinks; Greengage, a smaller accommodation, and the Bradshaw, a guest room with twin beds. Each is decorated in a unique blend of Victorian and country antiques with well-crafted reproductions. Some have armoires and wicker furniture. Nothing has escaped the innkeeper's eye. Even the nightstand drawers are filled with curiosities like fragrant sachets, a Victorian valentine, a postcard, a book of poetry, old spectacles, or a weathered copy of *The Farmer's Almanac*.

Chocolate-chip muffins or Sandy's peach coffee cake often highlight the generous continental breakfast eaten in the dining room or on the enclosed porch. Through the tall arched windows you can look out over small garden areas, and across acres of fields and woodlands.

Ninety miles from Niagara Falls, and just twelve miles from Lake Erie, Plumbush is less than a mile from the world-famous Chautauqua Institution, to whose lectures, study groups, opera, dance, and numerous musical events people flock every summer.

PLUMBUSH, Chautauqua-Stedman Road, Box 332, RD 2, Mayville, NY 14757; (716) 789-5309; Sandy and George Green, owners. Open all year. Four guest rooms with private baths. Rates: $65 to $85 double, including expanded continental breakfast. Children 12 and over welcome; no pets; smoking outside only; Visa/MasterCard. Recommended dining at The Curly Maple, Webb's, Chautauqua Publick Inn. Cross-country and downhill skiing and snowmobiling in winter. Golf, sailing, in summer.

DIRECTIONS: from Rte. 17 take exit 7 onto Rte. 33 north for 3 miles.

CAPTAIN SCHOONMAKER'S

Gastronomical breakfasts

The 1760 stone house on the Kriegs' property is the main house, but is only one of three accommodating structures that comprise Captain Schoonmaker's. Just beyond the driveway sits a whimsically restored barn, where the most asked-after rooms look out over the brook. The other most often-requested rooms are hidden away down the street in the old canal lock-tender's quarters. Guests have to walk the half mile from the canal-side cottage to the main house, but it's a welcome activity after Julia Krieg's amazingly ample breakfast.

Talkative and perky, hostess Julia won't take no for an answer. Her guests groan with surfeited delight by the fourth course at breakfast. Saturday's usual menu begins with broiled grapefruit and moves on to an herb-cheese soufflé accompanied by sausage almost candied with New York maple syrup. The meal continues with a halo of apricot and honey Danish. Is breakfast over? No; with theatrical timing, Julia again appears: this time with cherry strudel. Hence, the groan.

CAPTAIN SCHOONMAKER'S 1760 STONE HOUSE, Box 37, Route 237, High Falls, NY 12440; (914) 687-7946; Sam and Julia Krieg, hosts. Open year-round. Three guests rooms in the main stone house, four rooms in the carriage house/barn, four rooms in the Towpath House; all with private or shared baths. Two rooms with fireplace. Rates: $75 and $85. Full breakfast. Children welcome during the week, over 6 only, on weekends; no pets; no credit cards. Hiking, boating, tubing, swimming, horseback riding, golf, wineries, summer theater nearby.

DIRECTIONS: from Kingston take Rte. 209W to Ellenville to 213E to Rosendale (left turn), about 3 miles to the house, which is on the right. Sam will pick guests up at the bus station in Rosendale.

MAPLE SHADE BED & BREAKFAST

A country oasis

Hidden away in some of New York's most beautiful countryside, Cooperstown sits on the shores of scenic Lake Otsego. There's nothing pretentious about this sophisticated back-country oasis. The small shopping district is well-organized to fend off insensitive developers, and so Main Street flourishes as it did years ago with stores and a 1920s movie theatre. Even the National Baseball Hall of Fame hasn't intruded on the town's quiet sense of pride and practicality.

Judge William Cooper settled here in 1786 and built the village's first two log structures. His son, James Fenimore, immortalized the area in his books.

The tone is casual and friendly. White and pastel colors define the American country theme, and set off the slate blue carpeting. Old oak, new brass, and wicker blend together into a pleasing package presided over by congenial hosts Robert and Linda Crampton, natives of the area.

MAPLE SHADE BED AND BREAKFST, R.D. #1, Box 105A, Milford, NY 13807; (607) 547-9530; Robert and Linda Crampton, hosts. Open all year. Three guest rooms share two baths; one suite has private bath. Rates: $55 to $65; $5 additional per person; includes hearty breakfast. Children allowed, no pets; no smoking; no credit cards, personal checks. Good restaurants are abundant.

DIRECTIONS: from the south, take the New York State Thruway to exit 21 (Catskill) to Rte. 145 north. Turn onto Rte. 20 west, then Rte. 28 south through Cooperstown. The inn is four miles from town, on the right. From I-88, take Rte. 28 north. The inn is on the left.

The house is colorful, gay, and fanciful.

UJJALA'S BED & BREAKFAST

A bit of California in upstate New York

Ujjala's Bed and Breakfast vibrates with a California sensibility. Her charming Victorian frame cottage sits amidst a grove of apple, pear, and quince trees, and is painted in luscious hues of lilac, periwinkle, and plum. Ujjala renovated her home and added skylights, contemporary stained glass, lots of plants, whimsical ceramics, and flowers.

The focus at Ujjala's is on health. With a background in "body therapy"—Shiatsu and deep-relaxation therapy—she has given courses in stress management to university students and corporate business people, and she was filmed for the television special "The Body Human." Ujjala is also an able cook who specializes in "vegetarian gourmet" cuisine. Her full breakfast includes homemade whole grain breads, fresh fruits, and eggs, and she goes out of her way to accommodate people on special diets. If you've

always wanted to cleanse your system with a fast or a special diet, a stay at Ujjala's may be in order. Link a well-balanced and healthful diet with Ujjala's therapy and you can come away from this bed and breakfast feeling like a brand new person.

UJJALA'S BED AND BREAKFAST , 2 Forest Glen Rd., New Paltz, NY 12561; (914) 255-6360; Ujjala Schwartz, hostess. Open all year. Five guest rooms with private and shared baths. Rates $65 to $85 double, including full breakfast. Afternoon tea and coffee, sherry in winter. Excellent dining nearby. Inquire about children; no pets; smoking discouraged; no credit cards. Inn offers exercise and relaxation therapy programs.

DIRECTIONS: from N.Y. State Thruway, take New Paltz Exit 18. Go left on Rte. 299 into town and turn left at light onto Rte. 208 S. Drive 3½ miles, passing Dressel Farm on right, take second right onto Forest Glen Rd. Ujjala's is driveway on left.

STAGECOACH INN

Its own brand of romance

Bustling Lake Placid Village lies tucked between two shimmering bodies of water. Shallow and tranquil Mirror Lake laps up to the town's center. Just a few miles north, Lake Placid serves as the village's reservoir, reaching spring-fed depths of over 300 feet—an angler's paradise with native fish as well as upwards of 10,000 rainbow and lake trout stocked by the state each year.

Sports activities are a large part of village life. Many of the 1980 Winter Olympic structures continue to bring in world-class championships throughout the year.

The 1833 clapboard Stagecoach Inn sits two miles northwest of the ski jumps on a back street away from traffic and village noise. Rustic and casual, the inn delivers its own brand of romance to its guests. Warmed by a fireplace, the two-story cathedral-ceilinged living room invites sitting back and enjoying the Adirondack-style details that once marked an era of extravagant parties and stimulating conversation. Yellow birch logs and twigs form the mantel, bookshelves, and support beams, as well as an imposing banister that leads to a second floor balcony.

The view down to the living room makes a still life *extraordinaire*. A deer head rests comfortably above the fireplace, a working Mason and Hamlin organ stands to the left, and on the side wall crossed snowshoes hang over framed photos of former innkeepers Mr. and Mrs. Lyons.

The other common area, the dining room, encloses its visitors with Georgia pine on the walls, ceiling, and floors. A cozy fire reflects in the wood's sheen, casting an amber radiance on the morning meal—a perfect touch to start any day.

THE STAGECOACH INN, Old Military Road, Lake Placid, NY 12946; (518) 523-9474; Peter Moreau, inn owner; Lyn Witte, innkeeper. Open all year. Nine cozy guest rooms, five with private baths, two with fireplaces. Rates: $45 to $70, single; $55 to $80, double; $15 for an additional person. Children over 10 welcome; inquire about pets. Sports activities nearby include golf, hiking, rock climbing, trout fishing, horseback riding. Skating school ice shows every Saturday night in session; Mercedes Circuit horse show in summer.

DIRECTIONS: from the Adirondack Northway (Rte. 87), take Rte. 73N for 30 miles. Bear left just past the ski jumps (where the Saranac Lake sign is pointing). The inn is about two miles down on the left.

Innkeepers Jack and Joan Grimes and their sumptuous inn.

THE INN AT BROOK WILLOW

A pastoral retreat

This bed and breakfast is a truly pastoral retreat. Passing over a brook and through a gate, you arrive to find an extended Victorian cottage and a reborn barn amidst hills of wildflowers and graceful trees. A small bottle of wine along with fresh fruit and flowers greet you in each room and a feeling of serenity sets in.

Hosts Joan and Jack Grimes fell in love with this rural area of upstate New York farmland. They left their old lives behind, and relocated here to follow their dream. As gracious and friendly hosts, they easily convince visitors to share their appreciation of nature and of nearby Cooperstown, an unspoiled Victorian-era town.

The red barn houses three guest rooms, each tastefully decorated in a mixture of modern and country collectible furnishings. The main house offers two more guest rooms as well as delightful common areas. A large contemporary living room provides a wide sweeping view of woodland and wildlife.

There's a Victorian parlor in the oldest part of the house, with an ornate, working pump organ for those who can play. White wicker furniture and a bird cage collection adorn the sun room, where light bounces in through many small-paned windows that beckon you to sit and enjoy the sunshine. The grounds around the inn are inviting, with lawns for lounging, and a swan-filled pond.

Breakfast is truly a social event, served at a round table in the Victorian dining room, where Joan and Jack often help guests in planning their day.

Cooperstown is most famous for The Baseball Hall of Fame, but be sure to pay a visit to the Farmers Museum, a seventeenth-century working village.

THE INN AT BROOK WILLOW BED & BREAKFAST, RD 2, Box 514, Cooperstown, NY 13326; (607) 547-9700; Joan and Jack Grimes, owners. Open all year. Five guest rooms with private baths. Rates: $55 to $75 per room, depending on season, including full breakfast. Children welcome; no pets; no smoking; no credit cards. Fine restaurants in Cooperstown. Baseball Hall of Fame, Farmers' Museum Country club privileges for golf, tennis, swimming. Skiing in winter.

DIRECTIONS: 5 minutes from town; call for directions.

J. P. SILL HOUSE

A showcase of wallpapers

Formal elegance betrays a studied warmth in the J.P. Sill House, a showcase of impeccably designed and printed wallpapers. The handscreened "room sets" may include as many as seven different yet harmonious patterns. All are based on original works by turn-of-the-century artists. The previous innkeeper, Joyce Bohlman, discovered the California firm of Bradbury & Bradbury from a newspaper article; an inquiry and a visit to the firm convinced her to paper the house with these carefully chosen designs. The results are spectacular.

The green-hued formal dining room carries an Eastlake frieze paper initially reproduced for the Cameron-Stanford House in Oakland, California; the fill paper, a graceful willow pattern, is attributed to William Morris. Both become richer when sunlight filters in through the room's French doors that open onto one of the inn's porches.

Joyce kept pieces of the wallpapers with her for six months wherever she traveled, buying material and accessories to fit the beautifully

Bradbury & Bradbury wallpaper in the Peacock Room.

appointed rooms, all of which are furnished with antiques to match the ambiance of the papers: an Eastlake bed stands at counterpoint to the green marble fireplace in the Master Bedroom; a brass and white-iron bed complements the soft peach and blue of the Shell Room. Linens and lace add to the details.

The house seduces its guests. A long tin bathtub invites visitors to take a luxurious break—bath powder already provided. Seasonal fruit baskets or homemade sweets adorn the rooms as appropriately as the objets d'arts, and potpourri scents the air.

Expect the same quality of attention at breakfast from the new innkeepers, Angelo and Laura. Simply prepared gourmet fare comes presented on china. White linen napkins and silver service complete this unabashed indulgence.

THE J.P. SILL HOUSE, 63 Chestnut St., Cooperstown, NY 13326; (607) 547-2633; Angelo and Laura Panicello-Zuccotti, innkeeper. Open all year. 1894 Italiante Victorian on state and national historic registers. Five guest rooms share 2½ baths; 1 suite. Rates: $65 to $150. Two-night minimum for summer weekends; 3-night minimum for holiday weekends. Full, elegant breakfast. No pets, kennel nearby; no children under 13; no smoking. Year-round sports activities: Lake Otsego; Baseball Hall of Fame; Farmer's Museum; Fenimore House; antiquing, auctions, summer theatre, and opera.

DIRECTIONS: once in Cooperstown, ask inn for location of the house.

ROSEWOOD INN

Unique character and charm

This 1855 Greek Revival mansion was transformed into an English Tudor in 1917 and is now a bed and breakfast, presided over by popular local newspaper editor Dick Peer, and his wife, Winnie. It is a first-class hostelry in the finest tradition.

Six guest rooms, named after popular figures, offer their own unique character and charm. The Jenny Lind Room features sheet music and programs from the Swedish Nightingale's concerts; the Herman Melville Room, Gloucester whaling prints and a harpoon on the mantel; the Charles Dana Gibson Room, Gibson Girl prints and Eastlake furniture.

The Corning Glass Museum, within walking distance of Rosewood Inn, houses the most extensive glass collection in the world. On display are ancient Egyptian, Roman, Venetian, and Persian glass, and a vast Tiffany window of a scene overlooking the Hudson.

The Rockwell Museum, also nearby, features the largest collection of Western art in the eastern United States.

ROSEWOOD INN, 134 East First St., Corning, NY 14830; (607) 962-3253; Winnie and Dick Peer, hosts. Open all year. Six guest rooms, four with private baths. Rates $65 to $100. Includes full breakfast. Children welcome; inquire about pets; smoking on side porch; Visa/MasterCard/Diners Club. Scenic Finger Lakes, Watkins Glen, auto racing, wineries, Ithaca and its universities within a short drive.

DIRECTIONS: take Rte. 17 through downtown Corning. East First Street parallels Rte. 17 one block to the south.

The Jenny Lind Room.

PHOTOGRAPHS COURTESY ROSEWOOD INN

JOANNE GIGANTI PHOTOGRAPHS

Sumptuously Victorian.

VILLAGE VICTORIAN INN

Romantic guest rooms

This cheerful yellow bed and breakfast inn sits on an in-town corner of the historic village of Rhinebeck. Guests enjoy a wonderful blend of old-fashioned elegance and 1990s casual style, whether inside or out on the porch.

The five bedrooms are quite romantic and wide plank floors and floral patterns accompany some extremely striking furnishings. Among them are ornate wooden armoires and a stunning gate-like nineteenth-century brass bed. Lace-curtained windows let sunlight shine throughout the inn.

A full breakfast is served at intimate, carved-oak tables in a dining room that shows off the Victorian mastery of fine woodworking, with fantastic inlaid oak and dark wood floors, and an eight-foot-tall, carved English-style bar. Animals and human faces appear among the intricately-worked curlicues, and a collection of cranberry glass sits above.

The village of Rhinebeck begs to be explored on foot, and has a lively assortment of restaurants, antiques stores, galleries, and shops. Also worth visiting in the area are the Vanderbilt and Roosevelt

Mansions, sitting grandly along the nearby Hudson River.

THE VILLAGE VICTORIAN INN AT RHINEBECK, 31 Center Street, Rhinebeck, NY 12572; (914) 876-8345; Judy Kohler, owner. Open all year. Five guest rooms with private baths. Rates: $165 to $250 per room, including full gourmet breakfast served at private tables from 8 to 10 A.M. Specialties include apple crisp, pecan-stuffed French toast, cheese blintzes. Children over 17 welcome; no pets; smoking in parlor and porch only; credit cards accepted. Numerous restaurants in village. Roosevelt and Vanderbilt mansions nearby.

DIRECTIONS: Taconic State Parkway to Rte. 199 west to Rhinebeck. Turn right on Center St. to inn.

JAMES RUSSELL WEBSTER INN

Two grand, palatial suites

Built by one of the Webster brothers of dictionary fame, and graced by a terraced courtyard, this ornately-decorated Greek Revival mansion is set in the glorious Finger Lakes region of New York state.

Two grand palatial suites in the James Russell Webster Mansion offer everything. Private entrances, luxurious canopied beds, marble baths and fireplaces, black-and-white harlequin floors—all exude elegance. Museum-quality collections spill over throughout and into the suites. For cat lovers there are more than 600 cat figurines—musical cats, a marching band, ball-playing cats, mom cats and kittens. Rare European clocks—grandfather, double fusée chain bracket, automaton, and lantern clocks—are on display. And paintings by noted artists of the eighteenth and nineteenth centuries are hung throughout the inn.

A breakfast of freshly-baked sticky buns, breads, pastries, fruits, imported cheeses, coffee, and tea are served on antique china with silver appointments, while a full gourmet breakfast is available at extra charge. Eggs Florentine, Quiche Lorraine, Nova Scotia, and home-baked bagels highlight the fare.

Candlelight dinners in the palatial dining room or in the summer dining house are easily arranged in advance. Gourmet-cook owner Barbara Cohen can furnish exquisite Veal Orloff, Poulet Dannielle, succulent glazed. duckling, and lobster overflowing with crabmeat. Desserts are too mouthwatering to mention in passing.

Local attractions include Seneca Falls, the Rose Hill Mansion with its boxwood gardens, the only Women's Rights National Park in the world, the Women's Hall of Fame, and a Scythe Tree, where farm boys hung their scythes as they marched off to the Civil War.

THE HISTORIC JAMES RUSSELL WEBSTER MANSION INN, 115 East Main Street, Waterloo, NY 13165; (315) 539-3032; Leonard and Barbara Cohen, hosts. Two grand palatial suites with enormous half moon windows, carved fan shaped mouldings, 12-foot 18th century Georgian doors, marble fireplaces, and marble baths. Rates: $180.00 per night double. Dinners $60 to $70 per person. Gourmet continental breakfast included, full gourmet breakfast extra. No children; no pets; no smoking; Visa/MasterCard. Delightful pet cats on premises. In the heart of the Finger Lakes country with eleven lakes, a thousand waterfalls, and fabulous fall foliage.

DIRECTIONS: Between Geneva and Seneca Falls. Exit 41 on New York State Thruway. Call for directions.

SARATOGA ROSE INN

Gourmet breakfasts

The Saratoga Rose, just 16 miles from the bustling resort towns of Lake George and Saratoga Springs, offers a romantic, turn-of-the-century respite in the rugged beauty of the Adirondack Mountains.

The late Queen Anne-Victorian, cheerfully trimmed in purple and rose hues, was built in 1885 as a gift to a bride. The skill of the original Adirondack artisans who built it is evident throughout the mansion, with its intricately inlaid and parquet wood floors, forty stained-glass windows, and an amazing terra-cotta corner fireplace in the entryway.

A lot of love—literally—went into the restoration of the home in 1988, when newlyweds Tony and Nancy Merlino bought and renovated it as part of their honeymoon. Two months later, guests began to arrive, and have been basking in their hospitality ever since.

The Merlinos were able to preserve or match much of the original wallpaper and filled the Saratoga Rose with romantic country Victoriana. Upstairs, five period guest rooms offer privacy and comfort. The spacious, blue Queen Anne Room is popular with newlyweds and honeymooners, with its wood-and-tile fireplace and quilt-covered bed.

Guests staying in the Garden Room may think they have found a little piece of heaven. Decorated in shades of green and cream, with a carved spindle bed, the room has French doors that open on to a private balcony with a Jacuzzi. Highly recommended after a day spent exploring the area is a mug of Tony's liqueur-laced Adirondack coffee from the bar downstairs, and a soak under the stars in the Jacuzzi.

Guests wishing for fine dining need look no further than downstairs, where Chef Anthony Merlino presides over a first-class restaurant. Guests may have dinner served in their room, or reserve a table in the romantic wood-trimmed dining room.

Breakfast specialties include perfectly done Grand Marnier French toast, with maple syrup tapped from a tree on the property. Another offering, eggs Anthony, was so appreciated by a guest that she dubbed it Eggs *Saint* Anthony!

SARATOGA ROSE INN & RESTAURANT, P.O. Box 238, Hadley, NY 12835; (518) 696-2861; Anthony and Nancy Merlino, owners. Open all year. Five guest rooms with private baths and one with working fireplace and one with private balcony and Jacuzzi. Rates: $70 to $125, including full breakfast in room or in dining room. Well behaved children over 12 welcome; no pets; no smoking in guest rooms; all credit cards accepted. All activities available locally.
  DIRECTIONS: available on reservation.

Innkeepers Anthony and Nancy Merlino.

A superbly detailed guest room that includes a fine Eastlake bed.

Historical comfort

Between Gramercy and Stuyvesant Parks, in an old landmark building that traces its history back to Peter Stuyvesant, this triplex bed and breakfast is pure delight. The streets surrounding it have been well walked by the famous figures who have lived here, such as Mark Twain, O. Henry, Anton Dvorak, and Samuel Tilden.

Shaded and draped in paisley, the oak floored parlor has sofas piled high with Persian printed pillows. A Victorian china cupboard, drop leaf desk, silver tea service, and an old railroad clock add interest and warmth. Breakfast is served at a round oak table under a floral crystal drop chandelier.

Whether you are nestled in the bright Mexican-yellow room with pink accents on the lowest level or two flights up in the space with skylighted gallery and access to the geranium-potted deck, you will be pleased with your surroundings.

The hostess, who is native to Manhattan, will knowledgably direct you, depending upon your interests. There is a constant blossoming of trendy restaurants in this newly energized area as well as the old standbys like Pete's Tavern, Sal Anthony's, Fat Tuesdays, and the Gramercy Park Hotel.

GRAMERCY PARK. Landmark brownstone building. Open year-round. Two guest rooms with shared bath. Rates: $65 single, $80 double. Expanded continental breakfast included. Children welcome; no pets; smoking permitted; MasterCard/Visa/American Express. Near to Gramercy Park, Greenwich Village, Soho, midtown. *Represented by Urban Ventures, Inc., New York City.*

NYC—GREENWICH VILLAGE

Sophisticated décor

The airy cheerful apartment has two guestrooms: a pretty floral bedroom/sitting room with Eastlake chest and mirror, where you can sit up in bed and survey Bleecker Street, and a den with highriser, shelves of books, a desk, and typewriter. Art work covers all the walls—movie posters, two surprisingly striking vintage Red Cross posters, and botanicals. A varied selection of greenery and a colorfully patterned rug add to the charm and warmth.

The hosts are so well liked that guests have been known to throw parties for them before leaving for home. An entry in the guest book reads: "I have a new home in a big city. I will never be lonely again."

GREENWICH VILLAGE. Modern high rise building with views of lower Broadway. Open year-round. Two guest rooms, with a shared bath. Rates: $65 single, $80 double. Continental breakfast included. Children over six welcome; no pets; smoking permitted; MasterCard/Visa/American Express. Close to Chinatown, Little Italy, Washington Square Park, Soho. Two toy poodles in residence. *Represented by Urban Ventures, Inc., New York City.*

NYC—UPPER WEST SIDE

Spacious brownstone in a dynamic area

A sense of spaciousness comes from the fact that this three-story brownstone townhouse is a single-family dwelling. The third floor guest rooms were once the children's bedrooms and retain souvenirs of their adolescence. Just off Columbus Avenue—the most up and coming neighborhood in Manhattan—guests are close to Central Park, the American Museum of Natural History, and Lincoln Center as well as a plethora of fascinating shops and wonderful restaurants.

UPPER WEST SIDE. Brownstone and brick townhouse, built in 1887, with goldfish pond in back yard. Open year-round. Three guest rooms, shared bath. Rates: $55 single, $65 double. Continental breakfast. No children under twelve; no pets; smoking discouraged. Close to Lincoln Center and Columbus Avenue. *Represented by Urban Ventures, Inc., New York City.*

Plush and lush.

NYC—SUTTON PLACE

Gilt
and elegance

This spacious Sutton Place apartment is furnished as one might expect—*luxuriously*.

Beginning with the marble-floored reception area, the rooms unfold to reveal an elegant décor. A well-polished grand piano, a Scalamandré silk setee, coral-velvet side chairs, a Chinese art deco rug, Louis XVI armchairs, pastoral and floral nineteenth-century oil paintings, and a rosewood game table all command attention. Gilt and elegance are standard fare, and a collection of all-white porcelain china, including Limoges and Wedgewood, is displayed on a coral background.

Two guest rooms, one quite formal and the other furnished in the manner of a den, have private baths appointed with black porcelain and marble fixtures.

A continental breakfast is served each morning by the housekeeper, who will prepare a full breakfast or do your laundry for a small additional fee. All this, plus easy access by taxi to Bloomingdale's, the United Nations, and the Russian Tea Room, makes this location both chic and desirable.

SUTTON PLACE. A luxurious apartment with 2 guest rooms with private baths. Open all year. Rates: $90 for the one guest room, $75 for the other, or $140 for both, including continental breakfast. Children welcome; no pets; smoking allowed; some French spoken; agency accepts Visa/MasterCard/American Express. Directions given upon reservation. Many fine restaurants on nearby 2nd Avenue. *Represented by City Lights Bed & Breakfast Ltd., New York City, (212) 737-7049. Fax (212) 535-2755.*

A richly decorative setting for breakfast.

NYC—GRACIE MANSION AREA

Hob nob
with the Mayor

Under the stewardship of a British executive and his charming family, this eclectically-furnished townhouse is just blocks from Gracie Mansion, the home of New York's mayor. It is convenient to the Guggenheim and Metropolitan Museums of Art, and to summer evening concerts overlooking the East River.

A large fireplace dominates the living room and the space resounds with the ambience of a hunting lodge. Add to that a solarium and a rotunda-like dining area with a hanging two-story chandelier, and the effect is completely elegant. English antiques are sprinkled throughout.

The guest rooms are decorated in sensitively coordinated Liberty of London fabrics and wall coverings. Adjoining the rooms is an unusual balcony/library with floor-to-ceiling bookcases and a sumptuous soft leather couch overlooking the rotunda, where breakfast is served.

This upper east side townhouse abounds with good taste.

GRACIE MANSION AREA. A townhouse with 1 guest room and a garden apartment plus another luxurious guest room available occasionally with complimentary French Champagne. Open all year. Rates: $80 guest room, $125 garden apt., $100 special guest room; all include breakfast. Children welcome; no pets; discreet smoking allowed; Spanish, French, some Italian spoken; agency accepts Visa/MasterCard/American Express. Excellent dining in area. *Represented by City Lights Bed & Breakfast Ltd., New York City, (212) 737-7049. Fax (212) 535-2755.*

A Greek Revival interior with intricate Corinthian columns.

THE BARTLETT HOUSE INN

Beachside Victoriana

If you have ever wished you had an old family country house by the sea, then this inn will suit your reveries. The Bartlett House is a spacious late-Victorian with the casual style of a beach home, the kind of place where antiques and sea breezes live in harmony. An extra-wide front porch greets visitors to the bed and breakfast, and the roomy dimensions are carried on inside. The front parlor sports Corinthian columns by its doorways and an ornately carved fireplace. A grand staircase leads to the two floors above, with light streaming in through leaded-glass windows.

Guest rooms are welcoming, with brass beds and white chenille bedspreads. Rocking chairs, patchwork quilts and patterned rugs lend a cozy feel to each room. Innkeeper Linda Sabatino has a great eye for small collectibles, and you'll see the evidence in the many small lamps, tables, and curios that give the rooms their character. And everywhere in the house, from the dining room on up to the nooks and crannies of the third floor rooms, you'll find seashells arranged on ledges or tabletops.

The Bartlett House is in the center of Greenport, a former whaling town on the quiet North Fork of Eastern Long Island. A beach is located at the end of the street, and sailing, fishing, and canoeing are all available. The village is perfect for strolling or bicycling. Daytrips to Shelter Island, via the ferry in town, are a popular activity, where a nature preserve offers hiking trails. Antiquing, tennis, and golf are also nearby. Innkeeper John Sabatino recommends a visit to some of the acclaimed vineyards in the area for tours and tastings. "But," adds your host, "the most popular activity out here is just relaxing."

THE BARTLETT HOUSE INN, 503 Front Street, Greenport, Long Island, NY 11944; (516) 477-0371; John and Linda Sabatino, owners. Open all year. Nine guest rooms, including 1 suite, all with private baths and air conditioning. Rates: $82 to $93 in season, $67 to $79 off season, per room. Single is $5 less. Includes full breakfast, buffet style. Children over 12 welcome; no pets; smoking limited; all credit cards. Variety of casual to formal dining nearby.

DIRECTIONS: Long Island Railroad and buses to town depot. Arrangements to meet ferry from Connecticut at Orient Point. Ask for car directions.

PENNSYLVANIA

FAIRWAY FARM

Added attraction: the only trumpet museum in the world

Fairway Farm's claim to fame is its proximity to "the one and only trumpet museum in the world," says Franz Streitwieser, the world-renowned brass musician and historian who founded the museum and opened his house to visitors. Since his children have left home for school, Franz and his wife Katherine have tried to create a European-style bed and breakfast in the tradition of southern Germany and Austria.

The most striking antiques in the household are the Bavarian hand-painted blanket chests dating from 1805 and 1846. A blue-hued bed made in the Black Forest, with a heart-and-floral motif is a bit younger but just as beautiful.

The atmosphere is casual and nonchalant. featuring a wood sauna, spring-fed swimming pool, hot tub, and asphalt tennis court. Guests are free to roam down to the gazebo or to the pond.

The real fun here, though, is next door. For a suggested donation of $3.00, Franz will take you on a personal tour of the museum, sometimes even unlocking a case to give a musical demonstration. Over seven hundred brass instruments fill the cathedral-ceilinged building, including hunting horns, echo instruments, and the world's smallest trumpet. The museum opens up for chamber concerts and lectures, and a musical event is usually scheduled in the gazebo.

Franz and Katherine will also guide visitors to the area's many activities. Ski areas are only forty-five minutes away; the Poconos, one hour. The countryside is rife with antique shops. You might say that a stay at Fairway Farm is a well-orchestrated, harmonious getaway!

FAIRWAY FARM BED AND BREAKFAST, Fairway Farm, Vaughan Rd., Pottstown, PA 19464; (215) 326-1315; Katherine and Franz Streitwieser, hosts. German, French, and Spanish spoken. Open September through July. Four guest rooms plus adjoining hallway with Dutch-style foot-to-foot twin beds. Private baths in all except hallway room. Rates: $45, single; $60, double; includes a hearty breakfast with farm-smoked bacon and fresh eggs. Children welcome with supervision; no pets; smoking permitted on terrace; no credit cards.

DIRECTIONS: from the Pennsylvania Turnpike, take exit 23 to Rte. 100 north. Turn right onto Rte. 724 and again onto Vaughan Rd. Follow the signs from there.

Left, a stunning display of trumpets in the museum.

PINE TREE FARM

An elegant country estate

If you are looking for a tranquil country weekend, that is exactly what you will find at the end of the oak-shaded lane that leads to Pine Tree Farm. Built of native fieldstone in 1730 by a Quaker farmer, it was one of the first homes in the area. Today, the farm is an elegant country estate situated on sixteen-acres of rustic Bucks County.

Owners Joy and Ron Feigles share the entire first floor of their wonderful home with guests. The solarium offers relaxation country style, with a stunning view of woods and pond. A terrace and a swimming pool and tennis court are just outside in the garden.

Rooms are furnished with colors and fabrics reminiscent of the eighteenth-century proprietors of the farm, but with all the amenities of twentieth-century life. One of the four guest rooms has a spectacular white-twig canopied bed. Ron's collection of carved duck decoys is displayed throughout the house and, says Joy, "We've had more than one guest become a collector after staying here."

As life-long residents of the area (in fact, Joy's family came over on the good ship *Welcome* with

Joy Feigles welcomes you.

William Penn!) your hosts are happy to share their knowledge and recommendations with guests. Nearby Doylestown offers fine dining, shopping, and art, as well as the unique Mercer Museums. Henry Mercer, a local gentleman-doctor, dedicated his life to a collection of early American tools, from adzes to zithers, now housed in a concrete castle.

PINE TREE FARM, 2155 Lower State Road, Doylestown, PA 18901; (215) 348-0632; Ron and Joy Feigles, owners. Open all year. Four guest rooms with queen beds and private baths; 2-bedroom suite available. Rates: $115 to $135 per room, including full breakfast at private tables. Open pantry for soda, ice, cookies. No children; no pets; no smoking; no credit cards. Farm has its own swimming pool and tennis court. Outstanding restaurants nearby.

DIRECTIONS: take Rte. 202 south through the center of Doylestown to 2nd traffic light. Bear left on to Court Street for 1 mile to farm.

Indoor-outdoor living.

HARRY PACKER MANSION

A spectacular wedding present

The age of elegance produced some of the most spectacular architecture of all time. The Harry Packer Mansion is no exception. "An architect used this house as his inspiration for the Haunted Mansion in Walt Disney World," remarked Patricia Handwerk, who, with her husband Bob, is painstakingly restoring the house, keeping the old ceiling paintings, gilt cove work, and other particulars intact wherever possible.

Many of the elaborate, ornate extravagances that characterize the house can be attributed to Asa Packer, the founder of the Lehigh Valley Railroad, who presented the mansion to his son as a wedding present in 1874. From the very outside the noble details begin. Minton tile paves the floor of the Corinthian-columned veranda. The main entrance's 450-pound, etched-glass paneled doors open onto oak parquet floors. The Reception Room, the only common area not furnished according to Packer's plan, sports a walnut mantel and red pine floors. The adjoining library boasts an intricately sculpted mantel of sixteenth-century Caen stone that came from a British manor house. Above the fireplace rests a handsome niche of rich mahogany that follows through into dark paneled walls and a solid-beamed ceiling with oak inserts. The bathroom off the library retains the original mahogany toilet seat, a delicate Limoges basin set in a pink marble sink highlighted by silver spigots. The effect is entrancing.

THE HARRY PACKER MANSION, Packer Hill, Jim Thorpe, PA 18229; (717) 325-8566; Robert and Pat Handwerk, hosts. Some French spoken. Open year round. Second Empire stone-and-brick mansion with cast iron trim. Seven spacious guest rooms, two with private bath. Rates: $75 to $110; carriage house with six rooms each with private bath, $295; includes a full, elegant breakfast in the dining room. Coffee or breakfast in bed on request. No children; no pets; smoking in common rooms only. MasterCard/Visa. Steam train and Victorian high tea on summer weekends, carriage rides on Sundays in warm weather; mule and horseback riding; whitewater canoeing; Lake Mauch Chunk nearby. Call for details concerning Mystery Weekends, balls, and other special events.

DIRECTIONS: from the Pennsylvania Turnpike Northeast Extension, take exit 34. Continue 6 miles south on Rte. 209. Follow signs up the hill to the mansion.

THE CHURCHTOWN INN

Special innkeepers

The Churchtown Inn, a splendid fieldstone mansion, is the most prominent landmark in this tiny village overlooking the pastoral, picture-postcard fields and farms of the Pennsylvania Dutch countryside. Built in 1735, the house was owned by prominent Pennsylvanian Edward Davies, a member of the 25th Congress and a state legislator from 1804 to 1853. Today, innkeepers Hermine and Stuart Smith and Jim Kent have furnished the house with personal treasures and warm spirits, making for a very relaxed and comfortable inn.

The Smiths' previous life—he was director of the Stuart W. Smith Singers, which performed in such prestigious houses as Carnegie Hall and Lincoln Center—offered opportunity to globetrot, and this rambling, three-story inn is filled with antiques, *objets d'art*, collectibles, and conversa-

The warm and elegant front foyer.

Left, Pennsylvania Dutch countryside viewed from the back patio.

tion pieces. In the first-floor parlors you'll find French, English, and American antique furniture, Italian woodcarvings, a Regina music box, and Stuart's grand piano. Guest bedrooms are tucked here and there on the second and third floors; antique bedsteads and Amish quilts are the focus of each chamber. A marvelous new glass breakfast room overlooks the Welsh Mountains.

Each Saturday evening guests are offered the rare opportunity to adjourn to a local Amish family's farm to enjoy a bountiful dinner, during which they may be serenaded by the family's daughters, who excel at harmonious religious hymns. Afterward, back at the inn, Stuart often regales his guests with a short piano concert.

THE CHURCHTOWN INN BED & BREAKFAST, Rte. 23, Churchtown, PA 17555; mail to P.O. Box 135, RD 3, Narvon, PA 17555; (215) 445-7794; Hermine and Stuart Smith, hosts. Open all year. Eight rooms, 6 with private baths, 2 share. Rates: $49 to $95 double, with full 5-course breakfast. Children over 12 welcome; no pets; smoking in designated areas; Visa/MasterCard; limited German and Italian spoken. Special events weekends, including Thanksgiving and Christmas, from Nov. 15 to May 30. Area dining includes Pennsylvania Dutch smorgasbord.

DIRECTIONS: going west on Pennsylvania Turnpike take exit 22 (Morgantown) to 23 West for 3 miles to inn. From south take I-83 north to Rte. 30 east to Rte. 23 east.

Well worth the visit, winter or summer.

THE HAWK MOUNTAIN INN

Paradise for birdwatchers

With stunning views overlooking the foothills of the Blue Mountain Valley, Hawk Mountain Inn offers the nearest lodging to one of America's foremost bird watching sites. Hawk Mountain Sanctuary is a 2,200 acre wildlife refuge where bald eagles, ospreys, broad-winged hawks, and other rare species have soared for centuries. Nature lovers and ornithologists from around the world, who observe these beautiful creatures, now have wonderful lodgings that blend the finest European bed and breakfast traditions with the American accent on comfort and luxury.

Built in 1988 by Jim and Judy Gaffney, the inn has eight guest rooms, each one uniquely furnished with eclectic post-Victorian pieces, including rice, pencil post, and pineapple bedsteads, matching comforters, carpeting, window accents, and armoires incorporating TV units.

A Common Room dominated by a large native stone fireplace has a bar and a library of classic books. Here is where sumptuous breakfasts are served, and offerings may include fresh eggs from the inn's chickens, pork roll, slab bacon, whole wheat pancakes, omelets, or waffles.

Local activities vary with the seasons, and in addition to bird watching, there is hiking on nearby Appalachian trails, county fairs, skiing, antiquing, steam locomotive rides, shopping at Reading's famous factory outlets, and dining at the area's fine restaurants—all in the heart of Pennsylvania Dutch country.

THE HAWK MOUNTAIN INN, RD 1, Box 186, Stony Run Valley Road, Kempton, PA 19529; (215) 756-4224; Jim and Judy Gaffney, owners. Open all year. Eight rooms with private baths, 2 with Jacuzzis, 2 with fireplaces. Rates: $65 to $95 single, $85 to $125 double; includes full breakfast and complimentary beer and soda on tap. Children welcome; inquire about pets; smoking allowed; French and German spoken; Visa/MasterCard/American Express. Dining room on premises; Pennsylvania Dutch cooking in area. Birdwatching, skiing, antiquing, shopping at outlet stores.

DIRECTIONS: from east, exit from Rte. 78/22 northward onto Rte. 737 and proceed 2½ miles to left turn and follow road 1 mile to inn.

Handmade beds and quilts in the guest rooms.

SMITHTON

Pennsylvania Dutch hospitality

In the mid-1700s Henry and Susana Miller were devout members of the Ephrata Community, a Protestant monastic religious group founded by charismatic leader Johann Conrad Beissel. As "outdoor members," the Millers lived by a more relaxed discipline than the majority of disciples, who were celibate and ascetic. The Millers' home, a sturdy stone structure that served as a tavern and stagecoach stop, sat on a hill overlooking the Community Cloister. The Cloister was a remarkably beautiful group of medieval German buildings constructed along the banks of the Cocalico Creek, where Beissel and his followers lived and worked. Although the community of believers declined over the years, the Cloister remains—as does the Millers' home, which is now an inn called Smithton.

Smithton is a warm and welcoming home, and Dorothy Graybill, a Lancaster County native, is the gracious hostess. In this inn guests are steeped in two centuries of history while treated to the the true spirit of Pennsylvania Dutch hospitality. Throughout the house, from the airy kitchen and adjoining dining room to the deluxe, two-story suite complete with whirlpool tub, they will enjoy the special attention that is given to wood, from handmade beds and Windsor chairs to hand-fashioned latches and hinges, their design taken from a Cloister pattern. The focal point of each bedroom is the traditional bright and cheerful, handstitched quilt—made by one of the local Pennsylvania Dutch ladies, of course. Extra-large, square down pillows, perfect props for a good read in bed, and soft flannel nightshirts hanging behind each door are just two of many thoughtful and creative touches.

SMITHTON, 900 W. Main St., Ephrata, PA 17522; (717) 733-6094; Dorothy Graybill, hostess. Rustic stone house built in 1763. Six guest rooms plus one suite, all with private baths. Modest extra charge for third person. Open year-round. Rates: $65 to $115 rooms, $140 to $170 for suite, third person extra (no fee for infants). Full breakfast. Interesting choice of restaurants in area. Well-mannered children and pets accepted only by previous arrangement; major credit cards and checks; must prepay in full.

DIRECTIONS: from north or south, take Rte. 222 to the Ephrata exit. Turn west on Rte. 322 (Ephrata's Main Street) and drive 2½ miles to Smithton.

BUCKSVILLE HOUSE

Hospitality and history combined

At the Bucksville House, history and hospitality go hand-in-hand. The inn is a handsome, creamy stucco house and is the most prominent landmark in the tiny village of Bucksville, which lies a stone's throw from the Delaware River and a short drive to the shops and restaurants that line the streets of New Hope.

In 1795 Captain Nicholas Buck built the original building and founded the village of Bucksville. In 1840, Nicholas Buck, Jr. added more rooms and established a stagecoach-stop hotel to serve travelers journeying between Philadelphia and Easton. Innkeepers Barbara and Joe Szollosi are carrying on this tradition of hospitality, and their inn is a little gem.

Guests feel immediately at home, embraced by the warmth of the surroundings. Throughout the inn Barbara and Joe have carefully recreated the colonial era, with additional contemporary comforts, and the house is spotlessly maintained.

In the morning guests gather around the dining room table to enjoy a full breakfast and to revel in the room's rich colonial ambience. During chilly weather the Szollosis stock the hearth with firewood which adds an extra note of cheer. The breakfast menu might include a casserole of savory eggs or eggs and sausages; bran-raisin-walnut waffles; fresh peach fritters, in season; homemade sticky buns or fruit bread; and assorted fresh fruit and hot beverages.

Guest accommodations range in size from the third-floor suite, which boasts exposed beams and a full sitting room, and the second floor Gold Room, which enjoys one of the inn's original hearths, to the intimate Green Room, which contains a winsome display of vintage toys that were Barbara's childhood playthings.

THE BUCKSVILLE HOUSE, RD 2, Box 146, Rte. 412 and Buck Drive, Kintnersville, PA 18930; (215) 847-8948; Barbara and Joe Szollosi, hosts. Open all year. Four rooms and 1 suite, all with private baths and air conditioning. Rates: from $95, with full country breakfast and home baking. Children over 12 welcome; no pets; no smoking; Visa/MasterCard/American Express, checks accepted. Croquet, horseshoes on premises. Fishing, canoeing, swimming, riding, tennis, cross-country skiing, antiquing in area, as well as many restaurants.

DIRECTIONS: from Philadelphia take Rte. 611 North through Doylestown for 14 miles to Rte. 412 North. Take left to inn for 2 miles. From New York take Holland Tunnel to Rte. 78 West to Easton, Pa. to Rte. 611 South through Kintnersville for 1 mile to Church Hill Rd. Take right for 1½ miles to Rte. 412. Inn is second house on left.

Ray Constance Hearne making breakfast.

SPRING HOUSE

"Back to basics"

Ray Constance Hearne, a gracious and wise hostess, restored this 1798 historic house with a deliberateness guided by a preservationist's philosophy: "Buildings should show their age and reflect their history". When Ray mentions "back to basics," she means antiques, feather beds, down puffs, flannel sheets, and wholesome foods. "I get eggs from chickens that run around outside and eat grass." A weekend here, riding horseback across the swales, matched with a trip to the nearby Allegro Vineyards and one of the locale's fine restaurants combines for an excellent cure for frazzled nerves.

SPRING HOUSE, Muddy Creek Forks, York County, Airville, PA 17302; (717) 927-6906; Ray Constance Hearne, innkeeper. Open year round. Spanish and French spoken. Four guest rooms, two with private baths. Rates: $60 to $85, including a hearty breakfast. Refreshment served on arrival. Children welcome; pets boarded nearby (reservations recommended); no smoking; no credit cards.

DIRECTIONS: from the east take Rte. 202 to the Pennsylvania Turnpike. Pick up Rte. 202 again at King of Prussia (exit Rte. 30 west) and take the Rte. 30 bypass. Go south on 41 to Atglen, 372 west across the Susquehanna, and a right onto 74 north. At Brogue, turn left at the post office. Muddy Creek Forks is 5 miles; at the bottom of the hill is Spring House.

MAPLE LANE

In the heart of Amish country

It's Marion Rohrer's touch that makes Maple Lane so special; she adds a homespun air to an otherwise modern colonial home. Pierced parchment lampshades glow into the evenings, when guests curl up in one of Marion's or her daughter-in-law's quilts. Similar coverlets are offered for sale in a nook on the first floor. If the Rohrer family offerings don't fit the bill, Marion kindly directs serious buyers to neighboring Amish farms.

Longtime residents of Paradise, the Rohrers own and operate a working dairy farm with about two hundred head of cows. Ed welcomes guests to watch the milking, and he invites children to help feed the calves. Guests and grandchildren are the Rohrer's hobbies, so Ed loves to answer questions about the farm while Marion keeps track of all the auctions, farmers' markets, and antiques shops.

This is the heart of Amish country. Although Maple Lane is not an Amish farm—three of its neighbors are—the Rohrers maintain a refreshing air of simplicity and kindness.

MAPLE LANE GUEST HOUSE, 505 Paradise Lane, Paradise, PA 17562; (717) 687-7479. Ed and Marion Rohrer, hosts. Open year-round. Four guests rooms with two baths. Modern two-story colonial within sight of a 1785 stone house and Amish farms. Rates: $50 to $60. Includes continental breakfast. Children welcome; no pets; smokers encouraged to use the outside porch in warm weather. Two-night minimum on weekends. Tourist attractions, shopping, antiquing, historic homes nearby. Pennsylvania Dutch restaurants in abundance.

DIRECTIONS: turn south on Rte. 896 from Rte. 30. Proceed to Strasbourg; turn left on Rte. 896 at the traffic light and continue 1½ miles out of town. Turn right at the sign for the Timberline Lodge. Maple Lane is the first farm on the left.

BEECHMONT INN

Breakfast is one of the highlights

Beechmont is a handsome Georgian townhouse, set a few blocks from Hanover's town square and just twenty miles east of historic Gettysburg. Built in 1834, when Andrew Jackson was president, the inn witnessed several major Civil War clashes, first when General Kilpatrick confronted Jeb Stuart and was forced to retreat down the avenue in front of the inn, and again when General George Custer pushed the Confederates back down through the center of Hanover.

Innkeepers Terry and Monna Hormel furnished their inn with a collection of antiques from the Federal period, befitting the age of the house, as well as a blend of assorted, comfortable period pieces. Two of the inn's three guest suites are located on the first floor. The amply proportioned Diller Suite, with queen-size canopy bed, working fireplace, and equipped kitchenette, is ideal for guests who choose to linger in the area. The Hershey Suite has a private entrance onto the inn's intimate garden courtyard, which is shaded by a century-old magnolia tree. Up the broad and winding central staircase, past a gallery of family portraits, are located the remaining guest rooms— all of which are named after Civil War generals.

The highlight of a stay at Beechmont is breakfast, which is masterfully rendered by chef Terry. House specialties include shirred eggs in bread baskets, a prize-winning homemade granola served with "quark" (a heavenly mix of yogurt, sour cream, sugar, and spices), rice pudding, Hungarian sausage strata, corn custard, and spiced fruit compote.

BEECHMONT INN, 315 Broadway, Hanover, PA 17331; (717) 632-3013; Terry and Monna Hormel, hosts. Open all year. Seven rooms, all with private baths. Rates: $70 to $95 double with full breakfast. Children over 12 welcome; no pets, Visa/MasterCard; smoking in rooms only; French spoken. Fishing, riding, swimming, boating in state park; 3 public golf courses and many good antique shops in area. Many German country restaurants nearby.

DIRECTIONS: on Rte. 194 on north side of Hanover.

BRAFFERTON INN

Restoration in historic Gettysburg

In 1786, James Getty drew up plans for a new village to rise from the fertile farmlands of southern Pennsylvania. On the first deeded plot was built a sturdy and handsome fieldstone house, designed with deep-set windows, large and rambling rooms, and walls up to two feet thick. As the oldest and most unusual dwelling in all of Gettysburg, the Brafferton Inn witnessed the life and times of this classic American village. The inn (then a private home) was called into duty during the Civil War, serving the community as a church when the local house of worship was pressed into service as a hospital. As battle raged outside the doors of the inn, a bullet found its way into a second-floor mantelpiece, and the wound remains there today.

Happily, today peace reigns supreme under the expert stewardship of owners and innkeepers Jim and Mimi Agard. The Agards spent two years

Hosts Jim and Mimi Agard.

restoring the house, adhering strictly to an eighteenth-century aesthetic, even commissioning well-known folk artist Virginia McLaughlin to paint a striking mural on the four walls of the dining room, depicting the buildings that made up early Gettysburg.

During renovation the Agards purchased the attached house, created a handful of warm, comfortable, and extremely attractive bedrooms, designed a light-filled atrium to connect the two houses, and a fine bed and breakfast inn was born.

Mimi is in command in the kitchen, serving up a hearty, hot breakfast each morning, and she has gained renown for her masterful peaches-and-cream French toast. In fact, so delightful and authentic is every aspect of the historic Brafferton, *Country Living* magazine featured the inn in a lovely article on Gettysburg.

Early Gettysburg is depicted in a mural in the dining room.

THE BRAFFERTON INN, 44–46 York Street, Gettysburg, PA 17325; (717) 337-3423; Mimi and Jim Agard, hosts. Open all year. Eleven rooms, 6 with private baths, 5 share. Rates: $65 to $100 double, with full breakfast; $10 extra per child. Children all ages welcome; no pets; Visa/MasterCard; smoking restricted to atrium off dining room. Inn is in center of Gettysburg, within walking distance to restaurants.

DIRECTIONS: right off main traffic circle in downtown.

DULING-KURTZ HOUSE

Creative American fare

If a home with two rooms to let is one end of the bed and breakfast scale, then the Duling-Kurtz House & Country Inn represents the other end. Unlike most inns, this pleasant, clean renovated barn provides such amenities as a telephone and videodisc player in every guest room as well as a heat lamp in a modern bathroom.

The appointments are crisp-looking contemporary reproductions that fit the time and reflect the style of the person for whom each room is named. The light and airy Dolly Madison room with a basket-and-floral paper highlights a white

wicker ensemble. The more sedate Betsy Ross, a room of deep maroon, features primitive country and rattan furniture. The blue-gray and gray color scheme of the James Buchanan room helps to establish a Federal feeling. There are fifteen guest rooms in all, including three suites with sitting area and convertible sofa.

The inn connects via a covered, pillared walkway to a 150 year old stone house with a graceful white enclosed porch on the first floor and open-air veranda on the second. Reserve in advance to eat in one of the seven intimate dining rooms that comprised the original house. Exquisitely prepared entrées include lobster and shrimp Duling-Kurtz, brook trout almondine, Mediterranean shrimp, and grilled breast of pheasant. For special events ask for the *ne plus ultra* Duling-Kurtz Room, which seats two or four in a windowed nook set off from the rest of the dining area with curtains. The $25 rental fee includes a memento of the occasion: silver napkin rings engraved with the celebration's date.

Continental breakfast on a silver tray with the daily paper arrives at your door at a preappointed hour. Freshly squeezed orange juice, croissants, and freshly baked muffins are house specialties.

The inn benefits from its central location—within an hour from Longwood Gardens and Winterthur to the south, Valley Forge National Park to the northeast, and Lancaster County to the west.

DULING-KURTZ HOUSE & COUNTRY INN, South Whitford Rd., Exton, PA 19341; (215) 524-1830; The Pickering Group, proprietors. Blair McClain host. Open all year. Fourteen guest rooms, all with private baths; suites available. Rates: $49.95 to $120; each additional person, $15; includes continental breakfast in room. Children welcome; all major credit cards accepted. Excellent dining in area and on premises. Tennis, golf, and regional attractions.

DIRECTIONS: from Route 30 east continue on through the intersection of Rtes. 100 and 30 for 2 lights to Whiteford Rd. Turn left to inn on right.

Oscar Hammerstein's personal estate, where he wrote many famous songs.

HIGHLAND FARMS

Memories of Oscar

Oscar Hammerstein, the renowned lyricist of *Oh What A Beautiful Morning* penned that song along with many of his other hits while sitting on the porch of this inn when it was his personal estate. The eighteenth-century stately gray-stucco home is now a distinctive bed and breakfast, filled with its own unique history.

Memories of Oscar Hammerstein are everywhere. Each of the four guest rooms is named for a musical, and playbills and sheet music are part of their décor. There is a comfortable video library where guests may view tapes of his shows. *The Sound of Music* is written on the floor of the sixty-foot, pear-shaped swimming pool (Why pear-shaped? Because it was Mr. Hammerstein's favorite fruit, of course!). And the sound of *his* music accompanies breakfast, served with antique silverware in the former music room.

Breakfast is a sumptuous four-course event, served on the outdoor patio in warm weather. A special afternoon treat is presented daily between 5 and 6 o'clock: a pitcher of Highland Farms drinks (a creamy, citrusy wine punch) along with homemade crackers or hot roasted nuts. Served poolside, weather permitting, it is a perfect transition into evening on this peaceful countryside estate.

Mary Schnitzer's talents are not limited to her marvelous hospitality and cooking. Her handpainted motifs are in many of the rooms, including a horse on the wall of the Carousel Room.

HIGHLAND FARMS, 70 East Road, Doylestown, PA 18901; (215) 340-1354; Mary Schnitzer, owner. Open all year. Four rooms, 2 with private baths and 2 semi-private. Rates: $98 to $150 double, including full, 4-course breakfast and special afternoon treats. Children over 12 welcome; no pets; smoking in library only; Visa/MasterCard. Swimming pool and tennis courts on property. Wonderful dining in area. Great variety of Bucks County activities.

DIRECTIONS: inquire when making reservations.

Roughing it, Philadelphia style.

An original Eames chair in the guest room.

PHILADELPHIA—NORTH

A back-garden greenhouse becomes a fantasy cottage

Decorated with a light and casual hand, this combination greenhouse-and-potting-shed cottage is so inviting that many guests simply disappear for days on end, succumbing to the intimacy of the setting. The cottage shares a broad expanse of lawn with the main house and is bordered on one side by a picturesque grape arbor, and on the other by a large swimming pool. Only twenty-five minutes from Center City, this fantasy cottage is an ideal romantic getaway.

NORTH PHILADELPHIA. Private cottage, a combination greenhouse and potting shed, on three acres. Open year-round. One guest room (the potting shed), private bath (greenhouse). Rates: $90 one or two people. Continental breakfast can be fixed from ample supplies in refrigerator. No facilities for young children. Swimming pool on premises; stable, tennis, golf nearby. *Represented by Bed & Breakfast of Philadelphia, Philadelphia, PA.*

PHILADELPHIA—NEWMARKET

Federal townhouse near Society Hill

Poised between Society Hill and NewMarket, visitors to the newly restored areas of "historic Philadelphia" couldn't ask for a more convenient location. Meticulously renovated, this 1811 Federal townhouse beautifully weds mellow woodwork, exposed beams and brickwork, a pine floor, and working fireplaces with contemporary furnishings. The popular NewMarket shopping and dining complex is visible through the French doors in the guest bedroom.

NEWMARKET. Federal-style home built in 1810, with contemporary décor. Open year-round. Two guest rooms, with private baths, one with working fireplace. Rates: $60 single, $65 double. Hearty continental breakfast; guests may prepare full breakfast if they wish. No children; no pets. In NewMarket area, within walking distance of the historic district. *Represented by Bed & Breakfast of Philadelphia, Philadelphia, PA.*

PHILADELPHIA—VALLEY FORGE

An ageless colonial beauty

This large stone colonial is an ageless beauty of the pre-Revolutionary period. Nestled on four acres of magnificently wooded land, its title deeds can be traced back to William Penn in 1681.

The original part of the house was built before 1720. Two additions built later create the overall traditional colonial appearance. The last addition was completed in 1791.

Over the years, interior walls have been added and removed, but the original random width plank flooring, with hand-forged nails, remains. The old wood floors, fireplaces, stone walls, and stone smoke house were there when George Washington was at Valley Forge.

A highlight of a stay here is the full English-style breakfast, graciously served in the old part of the house in front of the colonial fireplace with a huge mantel and eight-foot-wide hearth.

Two guest rooms occupy the entire third floor, providing spacious privacy for couples or families. The rose and grey room has a canopied queen-sized bed. The second chamber exudes a fresh "peaches and cream" Victorian look and has an antique double brass bed and a twin bed.

VALLEY FORGE . Open year-round. Three guest rooms, each with a private bath. Rates: $55 single, $70 double; $5 extra for single night. Hearty gourmet full breakfast included. Children welcome; cradle and crib available; $5 pet charge; smoking permitted; guest refrigerator provided; pool in back yard. Five minutes to Valley Forge Park, one-half hour to Philadelphia. *Represented by Bed & Breakfast of Philadelphia, Philadelphia, PA.*

Breakfast is served in the pre-1720 part of the house.

WEDGWOOD INN

Where you can learn all about B & B's

The Wedgwood Inn was built on the foundation of "the old hip roof house" where General Alexander, Lord Stirling, stayed during the Revolutionary War. It is therefore fitting that the inn was recently designated to participate in New Hope's celebration of Washington's crossing the Delaware.

Situated two miles from that site, the inn is just four blocks from the center of New Hope. Named after Josiah Wedgwood, many of the inn's rooms have a blue and white theme. An ever-growing collection of Wedgwood porcelain is scattered throughout the house and a whatnot in the parlor displays among other things, a tea set from Queen Elizabeth's coronation, Jasper ware, and a commemorative bicentennial piece.

Guest rooms are comfortably furnished with period pieces. Cubist and Abstract paintings by Nadine's great-aunt combine favorably with a collection of contemporary crafts pieces to create an interesting effect.

In addition to running the inn, Carl and Nadine offer prospective innkeepers week-long seminars in running an inn or bed and breakfast. Everything is covered, from locating and financing a place to checking in guests, and candidates are given an opportunity to test the waters.

Extras at the Wedgwood include breakfast in bed, an afternoon fireside tea, Carl's homemade almond liqueur, and a complimentary ride into town in a Pennsylvania Dutch horse-drawn buggy.

WEDGWOOD INN, 111 West Bridge Street, New Hope, PA 18938; (215) 862-2570; Carl Glassman and Nadine Silnutzer, hosts. Open year-round. Twelve guest rooms including two suites, all with private baths; carriage house with private bath, deck, and kitchenette. Rates: $90 to $120 for room with private bath; breakfast and afternoon tea. Inquire for rates on suites and carriage house. Children accepted, call in advance; pets permitted, call in advance; no smoking; personal checks, travelers checks, cash. Two blocks from center of New Hope.

DIRECTIONS: from I-95 take the New Hope exit and proceed north 10 miles to the center of town. Turn left at the traffic light (only one in town) and continue up hill for 3 blocks. Wedgwood is at top of hill on left.

BARLEY SHEAF FARM

Romance and charm for blithe spirits

A sense that all's right with the world is the hallmark of the best inns. Barley Sheaf Farm in Bucks County emanates that wonderful feeling of security and comfort.

The property has attracted blithe and sophisticated spirits throughout its life, most notably when it was owned by playwright George S. Kaufman, and weekend guests included Moss Hart, Lillian Hellman, S.J. Perlman, and Alexander Woollcott.

Today, Ann and Don Mills' guests may stay in the farmhouse or in one of three bedrooms in the converted ice house. Bedrooms in the main house vary in size, but total charm is assured in each. A two-room suite furnished with an impressive brass sleigh bed, broad and comfortable upholstered couch, working fireplace, and French doors with handpainted privacy screen is the largest bedchamber. The separate ice house, comprising a living room with three very individual, country-style bedrooms, is tailor-made for couples traveling together.

A great percentage of the foodstuffs for a truly splendid breakfast come from the farm; the Millses raise chickens, keep bees, and harvest a large crop of raspberries each year. A puffy soufflé made from fresh eggs, buttery biscuits dripping with Barley Sheaf honey, feather-light pancakes and fresh raspberry sauce garnished with nutmeg-flecked sour cream, a homemade sausage ring, apple crêpes filled with cheese, nuts, and raisins and napped with homemade apple syrup, a sour cream coffee cake—need one say more to describe total satisfaction?

BARLEY SHEAF FARM, Box 10, Rte. 202, Holicong, PA 18928; (215) 794-5104; Ann and Don Mills, and Don Mills, Jr., hosts. French spoken by Ann. Open all year except Christmas week. Six guest rooms in main house, plus three in cottage; private baths. Rates: $110 to $175, $17 per extra person. Full breakfast served. Wide selection of restaurants in area. No children under eight; no pets; checks accepted.

DIRECTIONS: from Philadelphia, take I-95 north to exit 332 (Newtown). Turn left at exit and drive to fifth light, turning right onto Rte. 532. Take first left at Goodnoes Restaurant and then turn right onto Rte. 413 north. Follow 413 for about twelve minutes and turn right at intersection of Rte. 202. Farm is on the right about a five-minute drive on 202.

THE WHITEHALL INN

A handsome estate in Bucks County

Bucks County is blessed with lush countryside filled with handsome estates that have sheltered generations of landed gentry. And no Bucks County estate is more lovely than the Whitehall Inn. The inn sits secluded on a quiet country byway, yet it is nearby the center of bustling New Hope.

Mike and Suella Wass are the innkeepers *extraordinaire* of this 1795 great house, and their vision of hospitality would exhaust lesser mortals. A day at the Whitehall begins with a leisurely four-course breakfast, prepared by Suella and served by Mike. The Wasses' litany of gourmet breakfast fare is longer than your arm, fit for a four-star restaurant, and striking enough to be featured by *Bon Appetit* magazine. The meal is served on fine European china and crystal, but the real treasure is the Wasses' rare, heirloom sterling, passed down through Suella's family, which is placed, in proper English fashion, top-

Left above, the elegant breakfast table set with heirloom silver.

side-down to reveal the intricacies of the design on the backs.

These energetic innkeepers don't stop here. Mike makes his own bath salts, as well as fragrant rose-scented potpourri, concocted from petals gathered from his prized rose collection; and the Wasses attend to such details as providing each guest room with lead crystal wine glasses and a full bottle of wine produced by a Bucks County vineyard. Each day they prepare a sweet and savory afternoon tea, and they periodically host a theme tea, whose topic pervades the entire weekend. For example: a candlelight tea accompanied by Philadelphia's Fairmount Brass Quartet or by a trio from the New York Philharmonic; a strawberry tea or a chocolate tea, each attended by a speaker knowledgeable on the subject; a romantic champagne-and-candlelight New Year's Eve classical music concert.

THE WHITEHALL INN, RD 2, Box 250, 1370 Pineville Rd., New Hope, PA 18938; (215) 598-7945; Mike and Suella Wass, hosts. Open all year. Six rooms, 4 with private baths, 2 share. Rates: $120 to $170 double, with 4-course candlelight breakfast and afternoon high tea. Children over 12 welcome; no pets; no smoking; all major credit cards accepted. Swimming pool and tennis courts on premises, and dressage horses that accept carrots from guests. All of Bucks County's famous attractions immediately available, including restaurants, menus of which are available.

DIRECTIONS: from New Hope on Rte. 202 south go to traffic light at Street Rd. intersection. Turn left on Street to 2nd intersection at Pineville Rd. Turn right for 1½ miles to inn.

Each of the spacious guest rooms is furnished in a different period.

BRIDGETON HOUSE

French doors
onto the Delaware

Bridgeton House sits on the banks of the Delaware River. This is an enviable position, for while many Bucks County hostels advertise proximity to the river as a drawing card, few can truly say the river is their backyard. Beatrice and Charles Briggs restored their seven-room inn with an eye to incorporating the river by installing French doors and laying a pebble patio that sweeps to the edge of the riverbank.

With Charles' talent as a master carpenter and Bea in charge of interior design, the Briggses completely renovated and decorated what was a derelict building, an eyesore caught between the bridge and the road. Today, Bridgeton House feels like a cross between American country-naive and French provincial style. Bea uses soft color throughout, Williamsburg shades of faded cobalt, muted mulberry, and clotted cream. Thick rag rugs and a collection of antique Oriental area rugs accent painted hardwood floors. Fine bed linens and puffy comforters please the eye and assure the traveler of a comfortable night's sleep.

Bridgeton House is a casual, but sophisticated environment. Before becoming innkeepers, Bea and Charles worked in Bucks County inns and restaurants, and their years of experience show. Always available, but never intrusive, Bea sets a relaxing tone. She loves to cook and often can be found in the inn's beautiful kitchen, which opens onto the entry hall and adjoining dining room.

Outside the door, the Delaware River affords many diversions, starting with its lovely sixty-mile towpath, which is perfect for hiking, cross-country skiing, picnicking, and jogging. Canoeing, fishing, and tubing enthusiasts proclaim the Delaware to be among the East Coast's finest rivers.

BRIDGETON HOUSE, River Rd., Upper Black Eddy, PA 18972; (215) 982-5856; Charles and Beatrice Briggs, proprietors; Barbara Paul, innkeeper. Built in 1836 as a private residence, this home also once served as a bakery and candy store. Open year-round. Eight guest rooms, four with river views and balconies, all with private baths. Rates: on weekends by room $85–$165, including suite and Penthouse with fireplaces. Full breakfast. Good restaurants close by. Children discouraged on weekends; no pets; no smoking; personal checks accepted.

DIRECTIONS: from Philadelphia, take I-95 north to New Hope/Yardley exit. Follow signs north to New Hope. Continue north on Rte. 32, 18 miles to inn.

The elegant entry hall.

THE INN AT FORDHOOK FARM

Burpee seeds branches out

The Inn at Fordhook Farm stands as a monument to quiet, old world elegance. Three generations of the Burpee family, purveyors of world-class seeds, entertained guests in this charming, predominantly eighteenth-century fieldstone residence. The tradition is continuing since Blanche Burpee Dohan and Jonathan Burpee, the firm's founder's grandchildren, opened the house as an eminently comfortable bed and breakfast.

Each of the five rooms, named for different family members, has its own appeal, although honeymoon couples tend to gravitate to the spacious Burpee Room with its colonial revival fireplace and private balcony or to the stately Atlee Room, accented with leaded glass windows, fireplace, and balcony. The smaller Curtiss Room is a cozy nook with slanted roof and gorgeous view of the grounds. Double pocket doors distinguish the Torrance Room, as sunshine, peach hues, and three mirrored closet panels enhance the Simmons Room. The linden tree outside is a "a favorite haunt of the hoot owl," says Blanche.

Trees form an outstanding backdrop here along with the numerous gardens, including former seed-trial beds. Daffodils carpet the lawn's edge in spring, while marigolds last until the first frost. Lilacs, wisteria, and perennials dot the grounds amid gingkos, sycamores, dogwood, magnolia, rhododendrons and azalea, all befitting the gracious home of one of the most famous men in seed history.

THE INN AT FORDHOOK FARM, 105 New Britain Rd., Doylestown, PA 18901; (215) 345-1766; Blanche Burpee Dohan and Elizabeth Romanella, innkeepers. Open all year. French and German spoken. Five guest rooms, 3 with private baths, 2 with fireplaces; suite arrangement available. Rates: $95 to $126; additional person, $20; 2-bedroom carriage house from $163 to $227. Full farm breakfast included; afternoon tea served on the terrace. Children over 12 welcome; no pets; smoking on the terrace only; Visa/MasterCard/American Express. Tubing, canoeing, rafting, swimming, tennis, horseback riding, ice skating, cross-country skiing nearby; Mercer Museum and Moravian Tile Works; antiquing. Excellent dining in the area.

DIRECTIONS: The Inn at Fordhook Farm is located at Rte. 202 and the 611 bypass, 1.6 miles west of Doylestown. From Doylestown follow Rte. 202 south past the hospital and over the 611 bypass. Turn left on New Britain Rd. (first road on your left next to Delaware Valley College). The entrance to Fordhook is ¼ mile on your left through two stone pillars. Follow the drive over the little bridge to the large stone house on the right.

Above, the Breakfast Room. **Overleaf, the grand house and sweeping lawns.**

ISAAC STOVER HOUSE

Whimsical splendor

One of the most opulently eclectic and delightful inns you will ever visit is the Isaac Stover House, a beautifully restored brick Federal-Victorian right on the Delaware River. Originally built by one of the seven Stover brothers, prominent area businessmen, it now belongs to Sally Jessy Raphael, the popular radio and TV talk-show personality.

When she bought the inn in 1987, Sally spared no expense in restoring it to Victorian splendor. Guests find themselves greeted by Victorian floral-patterned carpeting, faux marbling, silk moiré wallpaper, silken tassels, gilded mirrors, paintings, a *trompe l'oeil* ceiling border, tables, and photographs. To that, Sally has added her personal treasure trove of collectibles from years of world travel—everything from Indonesian shadow puppets and antique stereoscope photo cards to Latin American folk art.

The magic touch that holds it all together is *whimsy.* Each of the seven guest rooms has a theme. The Loyalty Royalty Room, for example, honors everyone from George Washington and the Daughters of the American Revolution, to Chuck and Di of the British Royal Family. The Emerald City Room is done up in rich Victorian-green, complemented by Wizard of Oz memorabilia and—the perfect touch of whimsy—a pair of old-fashioned ruby slippers peek out from under the bed.

A three-course breakfast is served by the fireplace in the formal dining room. Sue Tettemer, the enthusiastic innkeeper, often presents the meal decked out in vintage finery. Guests feast on fresh fruit salad, a homemade granola and fruit yogurt parfait, homemade breads and muffins, and hot specialties such as stuffed French toast in raspberry sauce. There is an opulent, carmine-colored front parlor for guests to relax in, an upstairs library corner with a TV, and a casual greenhouse room.

ISAAC STOVER HOUSE, River Road, P.O. Box 68, Erwinna, PA 18920; (215) 294-8044; Sally Jessy Raphael, owner; Susan Tettemer; innkeeper. Open all year. Seven guest rooms, including one suite; 5 with private baths, 2 semi-private. Rates: $150, $175, $250 (suite), including 3-course gourmet breakfast. Children over 12 welcome; no pets; no smoking in guest rooms; all credit cards accepted. Hot air balloons pick up at inn. Picnic baskets prepared on request. Fine dining nearby.

DIRECTIONS: from Rte. 78 take Clinton-Pittstown exit 15 and go left onto Rte. 513 south for 11 miles to Frenchtown. Cross bridge to Pennsylvania and go left on Rte. 32 south. Inn is 2 miles on right.

Left, the lush, ornate parlor.

Innkeeper Susan Tettemer.

Breakfast time.

NEW JERSEY

CHIMNEY HILL FARM

Countryside tranquility

Chimney Hill Farm was built originally in 1820 as a small, stone farm house, with a sweeping view of the Delaware River Valley and Bucks County, Pennsylvania. Over the years it grew into a country estate and is now a gracious bed and breakfast.

The tone is set upon entering the formal living room with its dark hardwood floors, traditional antique furniture, hunting prints, and collection of cut crystal. Guest rooms are similarly filled with a mixture of antiques and period reproductions. The Hunt Room, named for the lawyer who once owned the place, is cheerily done in traditionally patterned fabrics of red, coral, and green, and features an elegant canopied bed. The Campaign Room makes use of more contemporary fabrics on a gun-metal steel reproduction of the canopied beds officers used to take to war with them. Faux marbling on the walls lends an artful touch to this original room.

A favorite gathering place for guests is a large sun room, with light streaming in, or with the fireplace aglow. Gardens surround the farm house, perfect for a stroll, and families of deer sometimes wander within view of the windows. A full breakfast is served in the dining room at candlelit tables for two, or around a larger table for the more sociable. Delicious raspberry jam, from berries grown on the property, and a morning newspaper always accompany the breakfast.

A feeling of quiet gentility permeates Chimney Hill Farm, complemented by the wide views of the countryside. Popular activities include hot air ballooning and attending the annual Amwell Hunt.

CHIMNEY HILL FARM, RD 3, Box 150, Lambertville, NJ 08530; (609) 397-1516; Kenneth M. Turi, owner. Open all year. Seven rooms with private baths, including 2 kings, 4 queens. Rates: $105 to $150 per room, including full breakfast. No children; no pets; no smoking; no credit cards. Antiquing and shopping in New Hope. Downhill skiing at Belle Mountain Ski Area day or night.

DIRECTIONS: call.

CHESTNUT HILL ON THE DELAWARE

Old-fashioned and very romantic

Visitors to Linda and Rob Castagna's home, Chestnut Hill, are enveloped by the warmth of the atmosphere and the beauty of the setting on the banks of the Delaware.

Bedrooms are old-fashioned and very romantic, thanks to Linda's gift for color and design and her many small touches. On the door of each room hangs a delicate wreath, and inside a handcrafted cloth basket is filled with fresh fruit in season. One room, entitled Peaches and Cream, is an aptly named chamber with soft peach-striped wallpaper, puffy peach comforter draped with a lace coverlet, and an oak chest of drawers and armoire. The Pineapple Room, which was the servants quarters, is roomy and private at the rear of the second floor. Decorated in cream, yellows, and greens, the room offers a bed dressed with a luxurious Welsh duvet and a wall of built-in drawers and cabinets in which hides a television. Bayberry features a bay window fitted with original shutters and is decorated in sprightly primary shades taken from colors in the bed's antique quilt.

Up a steep staircase to the attic suite, the bridal favorite, guests are in a world of their own. One bedroom is named Teddy's Place and contains several furry bears and a Little Golden Book of the *Three Bears* tale. Against a warm and rosy red print wallpaper, white eyelet and ruffled bedclothes look crisp and inviting. The bathroom, which displays beautiful Italian tile work, overlooks the swift-flowing Delaware.

CHESTNUT HILL ON THE DELAWARE, 63 Church St., Milford, NJ 08848; (201) 995-9761; Linda and Rob Castagna, hosts. Victorian house built in 1860, with gallery/gift shop on premises. Open year-round. Five guest rooms, shared and private baths. Rates: $70 to $95, $140 suite. Full breakfast served. Excellent dining in area. No pets; no smoking; checks accepted.

DIRECTIONS: from Milford, turn right at light and right again on Church St. (1 street before Delaware River bridge). Turn left into dead-end, which is Chestnut Hill's parking area.

Innkeepers Pam Venosa and Al Scott.

THE CABBAGE ROSE INN

As fanciful as a wedding cake

Splendidly asymmetrical, this Queen Anne Victorian presides over Main Street like a fanciful wedding cake. This seems appropriate, as owners Pam Venosa and Al Scott were themselves married here in 1988, the day before they opened the restored mansion as a bed and breakfast. Today it is the ideal return-to-the-past getaway, with pink and white gingerbread trim, and a high ceilinged, golden hued parlor.

Pam and Al lovingly created a romantic atmosphere to share with their guests. In each of the guest rooms they made use of beautiful materials (with many cabbage-rose florals, of course!) and enchantingly eclectic Victorian furniture. The Primrose Pink Room has a free-standing, claw-footed, pink tub beckoning in the corner, with a fluffy robe hanging by its side. And the bright yellow and blue Morning Glory room, with sunlight streaming in through four lace-curtained windows, will convince guests that they are waking up in a field of daisies and buttercups. Every guest room has a complete

china tea set on a table, and guests may arrange to have breakfast brought up to their rooms. Not surprisingly, the Cabbage Rose has become a popular place to celebrate wedding nights and anniversaries.

A baby grand piano, covered with vintage family photographs, dominates the dining room. On Saturday evenings in the winter, guests might catch one of a series of classical music concerts or old-fashioned sing-a-longs hosted by Pam and Al. And of course, guests are always welcome to play a tune when the mood strikes.

Flemington is a relatively undiscovered area, only sixty miles from both New York City and Philadelphia. The center of town is a National Historical District, surrounded by rural scenery. Flemington does have a reputation for its extensive outlet shopping and over 150 shops (mostly clustered in two Colonial-replica villages) are two blocks from the inn.

THE CABBAGE ROSE INN, 162 Main Street, Flemington, NJ 08822; (908) 788-0247; Pam Venosa and Al Scott, owners. Open all year. Five guest rooms, 3 with private baths, 1 semi-private. Rates: $60 to $85 per room, including continental breakfast in room, on porch, or in dining room. No children under 10; no pets; smoking on porch only; all credit cards accepted. Extensive and varied outlet shopping in town. Golf, riding, antiquing, auctions, Bucks County browsing, and local wineries.

DIRECTIONS: call.

Left, bottom, a luxurious bath in your room is an unforgettable experience.

THE OLD HUNTERDON HOUSE

A guest list of celebrities

Directly across the Delaware River from Bucks County, amidst wooded hills and rolling farmlands, lies the village of Frenchtown, abounding in fine restaurants, galleries, and quaint antiques shops. Comfort awaits the traveler at The Old Hunterdon House, a striking old mansion built at the time of the Civil War.

Ornate Victorian and Empire pieces, burled wood bedsteads, dazzling chandeliers, and oriental rugs on wide-planked floors all meld harmoniously. A full breakfast, served in the formal Victorian dining room, is presented on bone china, with crystal, silver, and candlelight.

The house was formerly the residence of the Apgar family, owners of the nearby National Hotel. One of New Jersey's best four-star restaurants, the Frenchtown Inn, can be glimpsed from the Old Hunterdon's front parlor window.

THE OLD HUNTERDON HOUSE, 12 Bridge Street, Frenchtown, NJ 08825; (201) 996-3632; Gloria and Tony Cappiello, innkeepers. Open year round. Six distinctive guest rooms, all with private baths. Rates: $90 to $115; special single rate Monday thru Thursday $75; two night stay required if stay includes Saturday. Includes full breakfast. Enquire about children; no pets; no smoking permitted. MasterCard/Visa/American Express.

DIRECTIONS: from New York City take New Jersey Turnpike to I-78. Go west to exit 15. Turn left onto Route 513 to Pittstown. Continue on 513 to Frenchtown. Inn is on main street, ½ block from river. From Philadelphia take I-95 north across bridge into New Jersey. Take 1st exit (New Jersey Route 29) north into Frenchtown.

The Victorian furnishings reflect the Civil War vintage of the house.

PHOTOGRAPHS BY BILL BAKER

JERICA HILL

Restored to match childhood memories

When Judith Studer was a child growing up in Flemington, New Jersey, she visited this old Victorian home that belonged to her best friend's grandfather.

It had been built by a local businessman who owned a neighboring lumberyard, and no effort had been spared in fitting the generously proportioned rooms with the finest woods. Five years ago she bought it, by then in a state of total disrepair. Lovingly she has restored it to match her wonderful childhood memories of gleaming hardwood floors and finely polished intricate woodwork. The exterior has been painted to reflect her own vibrant vision of Jerica Hill—a vivid gray with burgundy shutters and soft pearl gray trim.

The guest rooms have been named after Judith's relatives who lived in the area. Period pieces adorn each of the distinctive rooms: wicker and brass, oak, antique pine, and formal mahogony furniture. Antique spreads, coverlets, and country quilts dress up the beds. Lots of family pieces and things gathered up from the area appear throughout. Each guest room is supplied with fresh flowers, fruit, and sparkling water.

Born into the hostelry business, Judith grew up with parents who owned Flemington's historic Union Hotel, across the street from where the Lindbergh trial was held in the 1930's. For more than four generations her family has lived and worked in the area.

If you were born to shop, the town is awash with better than eighty outlets including Flemington Furs, Calvin Klein, Villeroy & Boch, and Waterford crystal. Many are within walking distance. When you are tired of shopping, Judith can arrange for a Champagne hot air balloon flight or picnic tours of the wineries in the beautiful Delaware River Valley.

JERICA HILL, 96 Broad Street, Flemington, NJ 08822; (908) 782-8234; Judith S. Studer, innkeeper. Open all year. Five guest rooms with private and shared baths. Rates: $60 to $90 double. Includes expanded continental breakfast. No pets; no smoking; Visa/MasterCard/American Express. Two cats on premises. Hot-air balloon flights and winery tours of Delaware River Valley arranged here. Outlet shopping galore in Flemington's "Liberty Village." Bucks County nearby.

DIRECTIONS: from U.S. 202 traveling north or south proceed to U.S. 202/Rte. 31 traffic circle to Rte. 31 north off circle. At first traffic light turn left onto Church St. and proceed 2 blocks to Broad St. Turn right and continue 2 blocks to 96 Broad St.

The largest, most imposing guest room.

THE NORMANDY INN

Gracious privacy a block from the beach

Of all the seaside villages that attract vacationers to the New Jersey shore, none is more gracious than Spring Lake. Bypassed by the teeming hordes who populate streets, casinos, and beaches of larger resorts, Spring Lake emanates a special grace particular to communities made up of broad avenues lined with grand, tree-shaded "cottages."

Built in 1888 as a private residence and expanded in 1909, The Normandy Inn, which comprises eighteen bedrooms, sits one block from the beach. Size alone makes the Normandy feel like a small resort hotel, though innkeepers Susan and Michael Ingino, who live in the house year-round with daughter Beth, maintain a warm and homey atmosphere.

Breakfast at this inn is especially generous and delicious. Each morning guests seat themselves in the large dining room—a room of such scale that young Beth dreams of converting it into her own private skating rink. The written menu offers many choices. Besides the requisite juices, hot beverages, and cold cereals, the Inginos serve real Irish porridge, four types of pancakes, two sorts of French toast, six varieties of eggs, four breakfast meats, and Michael's fresh-baked muffins or soda bread. Breakfast is Michael's favorite meal, and as a chef, he sees to it that guests need eat but a sparing lunch.

The Inginos are avid collectors of Victoriana and have furnished each room with antiques and details from the period. Rooms vary in size, but each is clean and very comfortable.

THE NORMANDY INN , 21 Tuttle Ave., Spring Lake, NJ 07762; (201) 449-7172; Michael and Susan Ingino, hosts. Italianate Victorian home near beach offers casual comfort and thoughtful amenities. Open all year. 17 guest rooms in main house, 2 bedroom carriage house apt., all with private baths. Rates $93 to $131 in season, $74 to $107 off season, double occupancy. Includes full breakfast. Good dining throughout area. Children who enjoy quietude welcome; no pets; smoking discouraged; American Express.

DIRECTIONS: from north, take Garden State Pkwy. to exit 98 (Rte. 34). Proceed south on 34 to traffic circle. Drive ¾ way around and turn right on Rte. 524 east. Cross Rtes. 35 and 71. Rte. 524 then becomes Ludlow Ave. Proceed to end of Ludlow and turn right onto Ocean Ave., then first right onto Tuttle. From south, take Garden State Pkwy. to exit 98 (Rte. 38 E). Cross Rte. 18 and turn right at next traffic light onto New Bedford Rd. Take sharp left at second stop sign (Rte. 524) and proceed as above.

CONOVER'S BAY HEAD INN

The pearl of seaside inns

Beverly Conover's light touch and delicate sense of color reveal an exquisite aesthetic sensitivity that defines the inn—from the embracing warm tones of lavender and mauve on the first floor to the family photographs she has framed and placed in each room.

Every one of the twelve dignified bedrooms has a distinct personality. The brightest room is also the most dramatic. Splashes of red and green in the geranium wallpaper match the brilliant red of the table skirt and ruffled cushion on the white wicker settee. In another room, a smoke-blue and white Laura Ashley print on the wall is reversed on the chair upholstery. In yet another, a spool bed and curly maple dresser are paired with pink and lime linens, a green stenciled border, and a row of small porcelain ducks that nest on top of the window sill.

The views are equally impressive. The sinuously curved maple bed in one third-floor room is placed so that reclining guests can see the bay, marina, and yacht club. Reflections of the ocean gleam in other rooms. Shapely old-style shingle houses comprise the rest of the scenic landscape.

Bay Head captures the feel of a late nineteenth-century residential summer village. The few, quaint shops sell antiques, art wear, prints, books,. gifts, and clothing. Very little tells of life's more pressing necessities. "Which is as it should be," notes Beverly.

"I like to fuss. I always fuss over breakfast," Beverly adds. Inspired baked goods grace the table as beautifully as the place settings. Fresh-squeezed orange juice and cut fruit are part of the full breakfast served every day. Guests can dine in the sunny breakfast room, on the manicured lawn, or on the front porch.

Conover's is a classic among bed and breakfasts, the pearl of seaside inns.

CONOVER'S BAY HEAD INN, 646 Main Ave., Bay Head, NJ 08742; (201) 892-4664; Carl and Beverly Conover, hosts. Open all year. Summer cottage built in 1905 and located one block from the beach. Twelve guest rooms, all with private baths. Rates: $105 to $140 weekends (weekdays less) in season; off-season discounts; $30 for additional person; singles $10 less double rate. Full breakfast included. Tea served in the afternoons until May 1. Children aged 13 and up are welcome in July and August only; no pets; outdoor smoking; American Express/MasterCard/Visa. Lawn games; golf; tennis; winter sports on Twilight Lake; beach; windsurfing.

DIRECTIONS: from the Garden State Parkway, take Rte. 34 (exit 98) and follow signs for Rte. 35. Continue on Rte. 35 south into Bay Head. The inn is on the right.

Some of John Peto's paintings, including a self-portrait on the easel.

THE STUDIO OF JOHN F. PETO

A secluded artist's studio

Gifted in the art of still life, John F. Peto, who lived during the latter half of the nineteenth century, was an artist whose talent was to go unrecognized in his lifetime. Throughout his career, he was unfavorably compared to friend and fellow painter William Michael Harnett. In 1950 the tide began to turn when the Brooklyn Museum mounted Peto's first major exhibition. Thirty-three years later when the National Gallery of Art organized a retrospective that traveled from Washington, D.C. to the Amon Carter Museum in Fort Worth, Texas, Peto finally emerged as a major American painter, now considered by many to be a far greater talent than Harnett.

Peto lived his life in virtual seclusion in Island Heights, a quiet village along the New Jersey shore, in a house he built overlooking the Tom's River. He first designed a studio for himself, a spacious and high-ceilinged room with white stuccoed fireplace, white walls, and "Peto red" wainscoting. He then built his home, including seven bedrooms, around the studio.

Granddaughter Joy Peto Smiley, as ebullient as her forebears were reclusive, has opened her grandfather's home and studio to overnight guests. Rooms are furnished much as they always have been, unpretentious with an eclectic mix of beds, chest, and chairs. In the common rooms hang reproductions of Peto's most famous paintings, and the studio holds a small selection of his original works.

Whether dining on Joy's "ethereal eggs," fresh fruit, and hot popovers, or walking through historic Island Heights, the studio, filled with the strong and quiet presence of John Peto, is the most memorable part of a stay.

THE STUDIO OF JOHN F. PETO, 102 Cedar Ave., Island Heights, NJ 08732; (201) 270-6058; Joy Peto Smiley, hostess. Open year-round. Seven guest rooms, shared baths. Rates: $55 to $100. Hearty breakfast served. Variety of restaurants, including a wonderful seafood eatery, in the area. Children twelve and over; no pets; American Express, personal checks.

DIRECTIONS: take Garden State Pkwy. to exit 82 east. Pass through six stoplights. Two blocks further, turn right onto Central Ave. and drive ¼ mile; halfway up the first hill, turn left onto Summit. Drive 4 blocks and turn right onto Cedar. Inn is 2 blocks on left (look for sign "The Studio").

THE WHISTLING SWAN INN

Fit for
the society pages

In 1905, when the local justice of the peace finished building his gracious Queen Anne Victorian home, he threw a party that was noted in the society pages of the *Stanhope Eagle*. Almost a century later, the splendidly-restored Victorian is The Whistling Swan Inn. Thanks to its owners Paula Williams and Joe Mulay, it is once again fit for the society pages.

The ten-room bed and breakfast is located in the quiet town of Stanhope, less than an hour away from New York City. High-ceilinged rooms and wide hallways create an aura of peacefulness. Especially serene is the third-floor suite. Its bedroom, in the turret of the house, has a cathedral ceiling and a series of etched windows.

The décor is mostly country-Victorian, making use of rich colors and textures. Each guest room has a theme, such as 1920s era, or Oriental Victorian, and much of the furniture came from Paula's family. The ruby-red parlor is welcoming, with its player piano and carafe of sherry.

While each room has a private bath, a unique amenity offered to all guests of The Whistling Swan is *Tubs for Two*—a large sun-dappled bathroom complete with two deep claw-footed tubs, a selection of bubble baths, and an armoire full of fluffy robes. The innkeepers can help provide you with glasses for champagne, chocolates, or whatever treats couples wish to relax with while they soak.

THE WHISTLING SWAN INN, 110 Main Street, P.O. Box 791, Stanhope, NJ 07874; (201) 347-6369; Paula Williams and Joe Mulay, owners. Open all year. Ten guest rooms with private baths and queen beds. Rates: $65 to $95 per room, including full breakfast served buffet style. Children 12 and over welcome; no pets; smoking on porch only; all credit cards accepted. All outdoor activities available, plus special events such as jazz and poetry festivals and major musical performances.

DIRECTIONS: from Rte. 80 take exit 27 north onto Rte. 183 for 1 mile to Hoss Building and turn left.

Left, wicker wonderland. Above, the inn faces right on the water.

COLUMNS BY-THE-SEA

Salty seabreezes and sounds of the surf

The sound of the surf lapping a sandy beach and the heady scent of a salty seabreeze lull guests at the Columns By The Sea. This grand inn is one of the few bed and breakfast establishments in historic Cape May to rest on the water's edge, along a quiet stretch of private homes well removed from the bustling esplanade.

The exterior is an eclectic mix of styles pulled together by a commodious, columned veranda which faces the ocean. Entering the mansion, one is enveloped by its Victorian past, thanks to innkeepers Barry and Cathy Rein. When they fell in love with this grand relic of the gilded age they embarked on a thorough restoration, and the result is this authentically furnished inn.

One of the highlights of the first-floor parlor, which boasts a handcarved coffered ceiling and beautifully paneled staircase, is a collection of exquisite antique Chinese ivory carvings. Two dining rooms adjoin the parlor and they display a treasure trove of antique china and 19th-century prints and paintings.

Each morning guests adjourn to these rooms to enjoy a gourmet breakfast served on massive dining tables draped with linen and antique lace. Breakfast begins with fresh fruit and moves on to a hot entrée such as "decadent" French toast, spinach soufflé, or asparagus strata. Champagne accompanies the inn's Sunday meal, which often features a delectable cheese blintz soufflé. Besides breakfast, guests are offered an afternoon tea which might include the Reins' trademark iced coffee (made with both cream *and* ice cream) and such appetizing morsels as Chinese egg rolls or Mexican tostadas. To top off the day, an evening tot of sherry or port is accompanied by a home-baked sweet.

COLUMNS BY-THE-SEA, 1513 Beach Drive, Cape May, NJ 08204; (609) 884-2228; Barry and Cathy Rein, hosts. Open April to Jan. Eleven rooms with private baths. Rates: $95 to $145 double, with gourmet breakfast, afternoon tea, and evening treats; Champagne Sunday brunch. Children over 12 welcome; no pets; no credit cards; German spoken. Dolphin watching from inn plus all of Cape May's recreational activities. Ten minutes drive to Italian, Cajun, Mexican, continental, and seafood dining.

DIRECTIONS: at southern end of Garden State Parkway to Cape May, follow signs to beach and turn left at Beach Drive. Inn is between Baltimore and Brooklyn streets.

Left, fun and games, Victorian style.

THE ABBEY

Casual elegance

One of the more elaborate carpenter gothic houses in Cape May is a seaside villa built in 1869 by a wealthy coal baron who spared no expense in creating an architectural masterpiece for entertaining summer guests at the sea shore. Now transformed into a bed and breakfast of expansive proportions by Jay and Marianne Schatz, the building has been delightfully restored. The interior contains a variety of decorative Victorian wallpaper reproductions as a setting for a collection of nineteenth-century furniture and bric-a-brac that brings the period back to life in a charming way.

An adjacent building, The Cottage, was recently added to the inn. Built in 1873 for the coal baron's son, it is a delightful empire style home with bright airy rooms furnished with choice antiques.

Croquet on the lawn, with the men wearing straw boaters; afternoon tea on the porch, including the hosts leading stimulating conversation with the guests; music played on an antique harp or an 1850 square grand piano in the parlor, which functions essentially as a music room; all these add to the atmosphere of life in another time—less hurried, less hectic, less harrowing.

Cape May is the nation's oldest seaside resort, and a stroll along its tree-lined, gaslit streets at dusk on a summer's evening recreates the heyday of the nineteenth century: ice cream parlors, Sousa brass bands, bicycles, carriages, knickered boys, hoops, and the backdrop to it all, the incredible collection of hundreds of extravagantly ornamented Victorian houses built in Italianate and Gothic Revival styles, among which The Abbey stands out.

THE ABBEY, Columbia Avenue and Gurney Street, Cape May, NJ 08204; (609) 884-4506; Jay and Marianne Schatz, hosts. Open April through November. Fourteen rooms, all with private baths in two adjacent houses (some with air conditioners). Rates: $90 to $150 per couple; includes full breakfast in spring and fall, lighter buffet in summer, and afternoon refreshments through the year, and onsite parking for main house. No liquor served; guests may bring their own. Well-behaved children over 12 welcome; no pets; all smoking limited to the veranda; Visa/MasterCard/American Express. Croquet at the inn, seashore swimming one block away, and many other activities.

DIRECTIONS: in Cape May, turn left on Ocean street, drive 3 blocks and turn left on Columbia Avenue. The inn is one block down.

MANOR HOUSE INN

Engaging innkeepers in Cape May

Cape May's Hughes Street is lined with gracious homes and lush shade trees, and it is one of the choicest addresses in the village. To make matters complete, the street is centrally located, between the shops and restaurants of the pedestrian mall, and the ocean beach.

One of the most relaxed and engaging places to stay along this tranquil byway is the Manor House, ably operated by Tom and Mary Snyder. Juxtaposed with the gingerbread opulence of many nearby inns, the Manor House is comparatively modest and unassuming. This inn is a spacious, three-story Colonial Revival home, iced with weathered shingles, capped with a gambrel roof, and girded in front by an old-fashioned "sitting" porch—a favorite hang-out during the balmy days of summer. Inside, everything is spit-and-polish perfection,

MANOR HOUSE INN, 612 Hughes Street, Cape May, NJ 08204; (609) 884-4710; Mary and Tom Snyder, hosts. Open Feb. 1 to Dec. 31. Nine rooms, 7 with private baths and 2 sharing 1 bath. Rates: $60 to $145. Children over 12 welcome; no pets; major credit cards accepted; Pensylvania Dutch spoken. Traditional seafood and "creative cuisine" restaurants in area.

DIRECTIONS: from bridge into Cape May follow Lafayette St. for 8 blocks to Franklin and turn left for 2 blocks to Hughes. Turn right. If street parking is full, pull into driveway next to sign.

The Queen Victoria Room is appropriately regal.

THE QUEEN VICTORIA

Imposing Victorian on Cape May

The Queen Victoria ranks among the best of Cape May's many distinctive bed and breakfast inns. It towers on the corner of Ocean Street and Columbia Avenue, a dramatic green and maroon gingerbread cottage. Owners Joan and Dane Wells are perfectly suited to the task of pampering this Victorian lady. Before beginning a career as an innkeeper, Joan was curator of the Molly Brown House in Denver as well as the executive director of The Victorian Society. Both positions required a dedication to the preservation of old houses, a labor Joan truly loves. Dane is the perfect counterpart. Though a tinkerer and hardware store aficionado, his professional background in retailing keeps the inn's business side on an even keel.

One of the most attractive and interesting rooms in the entire house is the front parlor, which is

The inn building is shown on the front cover.

filled with the Wellses' Arts and Crafts furniture collection—that wonderfully subdued offspring of the gaudy Victorian age.

Bedrooms come in many shapes and sizes. On the first floor the Queen Victoria room handily houses a massive armoire, tufted couch, king-size bed, and petit point chairs. Several rooms on the second floor and all on the third are diminutive and charming. The Wellses carefully selected wallpapers to suit the spirit of Victoriana, each with jewel-like hues and intricate patterns.

Though Cape May is a wonderful place to visit, no matter the season, the Wellses favorite time of year is Christmas. To make the season more joyous, they organize caroling, fireside readings from Dickens, and workshop sessions devoted to planning the Victorian Christmas dinner and decorating the Victorian home.

THE QUEEN VICTORIA , 102 Ocean St., Cape May, NJ 08204; (609) 884-8702; Dane and Joan Wells, hosts. French and some Spanish spoken. Open all year, minimum stays vary seasonally. Seventeen guest rooms and 7 suites, most with private baths. Rates: $80 to $130 per room, $160 to $218 per suite according to size and amenities (rates lower off season), including full breakfast served buffet style. Afternoon tea. Excellent dining nearby. Children in suites only; no pets; smoking restricted; Visa/MasterCard.

DIRECTIONS: take Garden State Pkwy. to Cape May, where it becomes Lafayette St. Turn left at second stoplight (Ocean St.) and proceed three blocks to inn, on right.

In the heart of downtown Cape May.

CAPTAIN MEY'S INN

Graced with exquisite detail

America's oldest seaside resort, Cape May conjures by its very name, visions of gingerbread and wedding-cake castles-by-the-sea. Protected from progress by the Pine Barrens and acres of wetlands plus miles of fertile fields that yield succulent Jersey produce, the village retains much of the charm of centuries past.

One advantage for today's visitor is the abundance of lovely bed and breakfast establishments, each quite different in spirit and temperament. The three on these pages are a sampler; it would take weeks to exhaust all the possibilities.

Captain Mey's Inn is named for Cornelius Jacobsen Mey, of the Dutch East Indies Company, who explored the area in 1621 and served as its namesake. This solidly built, late-Victorian mansion is decorated like an old-fashioned valentine. Voluminous lace curtains and lacey privacy screens, called *horretjes*, frame the windows. A china cabinet filled with innkeeper Carin Fedderman's collection of antique Delftware, family portraits, a nineteenth-century bible, antique pewter and copper, and abundant knickknacks and bric-a-brac fill the first-floor parlor and dining room. Carin is from Holland, and her Dutch heritage, linked with that of Captain Mey, inspired her and partner Milly La Canfora to create an inn reminiscent of her home. Many small touches—a small Persian rug on the clawfoot dining table; a plush, purse-like tea cozy; and the decorative *horretjes*—are found in many Dutch homes and add a distinctive European flavor. The house itself is graced with exquisite detail from three signed Tiffany stained-glass windows in the inner foyer to leaded, diamond-paned, ripple glass windows that glisten in the wide bay in the dining room.

CAPTAIN MEY'S INN , 202 Ocean St., Cape May, NJ 08204; (609) 884-7793/9637; Carin Fedderman and Milly La Canfora, hostesses. Dutch spoken and some French, German, Spanish, Italian. Open all year, weekends only January through March. Nine guest rooms, private and shared baths. Rates $75 to $145 double, varying with season and amenities; includes full breakfast served by candlelight. Afternoon tea. Excellent dining nearby. Children over ten; no pets; smoking restricted to the veranda; Visa/MasterCard; parking available. Cape May offers beaches (beach passes available), sight-seeing, antiques.

DIRECTIONS: take causeway bridge (Lafayette St.) to second light and turn left onto Ocean St. Inn is 1½ blocks ahead.

An extravagantly wallpapered Victorian guest room.

HUMPHREY HUGHES HOUSE

A doctor's home

Open year-round and presided over by charming hosts Lorraine and Terry Schmidt, The Humphrey Hughes House provides gracious accommodations. Bedecked in Victorian finery, the grand house is stuffed with treasures that belonged to the Hughes family, whose place in Cape May history was secured in 1692, when Captain Humphrey Hughes arrived to become one of its original landowners. This house, erected in 1903, and home to Dr. Franklin Hughes, remained in the family's hands until his son, Dr. Harold Hughes, died in 1980.

The Velvet Room, a guest room which was formerly the medical library, still houses medical books and medical instruments in elegant surroundings of carved oak and ruby-red glass. Another of the ten guest rooms, The Rose Room, has rose-silk walls, a damask fainting couch, and original gas fixtures.

Velvet and brocade-covered furniture, Victorian sculpted figures, lace-covered swags, and a mahogany square baby grand, all fan the senses. Add to that the wonderful ocean views, an elegant breakfast, two crackling fireplaces, and a glassed-in sun porch, and you have the perfect setting for "ladies and gentlemen on seaside holiday."

THE HUMPHREY HUGHES HOUSE, 29 Ocean Street, Cape May, NJ 08204; (609) 884-4428; Lorraine and Terry Schmidt, owners. Open all year. Seven guest rooms and 3 suites, with private baths, cable TV, air conditioning. Rates: $85 to $120 double, $135 to $175 for suites. Includes full sit-down breakfast. No children; no pets; smoking on porches only; Visa/MasterCard. In heart of Cape May.

DIRECTIONS: follow Lafayette Street right downtown to Ocean St. and turn left to inn several blocks down on left.

The richly paneled entrance hall.

The first and most honored bed and breakfast in Cape May.

THE MAINSTAY INN

Bed and breakfast at its best

The heyday of Cape May as one of the premier resort towns on the East Coast coincided with the height of Victorian carpenter craftsmanship in the latter part of the nineteenth century, and Cape May has hundreds of finely crafted, exquisitely detailed gingerbread houses to prove it.

One of these, an Italianate former gaming house built in 1872, was restored to its former glory by Tom and Sue Carroll, who have made the Mainstay into the best known bed and breakfast in the East. Because of their painstaking search for authenticity in the recreation of Victorian interiors, their inn has become a highly respected and much-loved model for other innkeepers aspiring to recreate the same sort of ambiance.

The interior of the inn is a unique combination of lush, Persian and Oriental rugs, wonderfully decorative Bradbury and Bradbury period wallpapers and mouldings, elaborate details in the form of paintings, china, drapes, lamps, quilts, chandeliers, clocks, vases, and, finally, an overwhelming collection of Victorian antique furniture. Guest rooms contain giant beds with decorative foot and head boards, intricately carved wardrobes, dressers, and washstands with marble tops, and velvet upholstered chairs and settees. The public rooms contain more: giant pier mirrors, elaborately upholstered walnut and mahogany chairs and settees, and exotic divans.

Amidst this Victorian flamboyance, the perfectly modern young innkeepers maintain an air of calm and serenity throughout the two guest houses. Guests meet each other over the delicious full breakfasts and during afternoon tea, oftentimes served on the Mainstay's ample porch.

THE MAINSTAY INN, 635 Columbia Avenue, Cape May, NJ 08204; (609) 884-8690; Tom and Sue Carroll, hosts. Open mid-March through mid-December. Twelve rooms, all with private baths, Rates: $110 to $140 in season; includes full breakfast in spring and fall, Continental in summer on verandah; afternoon tea. No liquor served; guests may bring their own. Children over 12 welcome; no pets; smoking on veranda only; no credit cards. Croquet and swimming at the seashore are popular activities.

DIRECTIONS: 2 blocks from Convention Hall in the center of town.

MARYLAND

Innkeeper Thelma Driscoll in one of the restored, luxuriously appointed guest rooms.

CHANCEFORD HALL

A dream come true

Chanceford Hall is virtually a dream come true, since it embodies all of the attributes we list on the back cover of this book as reasons people like to go to bed and breakfasts—interesting architecture, fascinating history, friendly hosts, scenic surroundings, reasonable rates, and sumptuous breakfasts.

The affable but determined hosts spared nothing in personally restoring the neglected mansion to perfection. Michael even sewed the drapes and made the antique reproduction furniture in his workshop on the premises, while Thelma laboriously freed the exquisite, handcarved detailing throughout the house from accumulated layers of paint.

The large dining room, with its beautiful furnishings, sets the scene for exceptional breakfasts, but the hosts will also serve dinners there to inn guests by prior arrangement. Beside a crackling fire on cool evenings, five-course dinners are served with sterling silver, Waterford crystal, and antique Limoges china. Given enough notice, any menu is possible, with the ingredients even being flown in on occasion.

CHANCEFORD HALL, 209 West Federal Street, Snowhill, MD 21863; (301) 632-2231; Michael and Thelma Driscoll, owners. Open all year. Five guest rooms with private baths and working fireplaces. Rates: $95 to $115, including full breakfast. Special dinners served by prior arrangement. Children over 12 welcome; no pets; no credit cards (personal checks accepted). Swimming pool on premises; country club golfing nearby. Recommended dining at Evelyn's Village Inn Country Restaurant and The Upper Deck in Pocomoke City.

DIRECTIONS: from Annapolis take U.S. 50 down the Chesapeake Peninsula to Salisbury and follow Rte. 12 all the way to Federal Street through Snow Hill. Watch for sign on lawn of inn.

WHITE SWAN TAVERN

Stay the night in a comfortable museum

A stay at the White Swan is rewarding because guests can feel the care the inn has been given. The main floor contains three parlors, or sitting rooms. The formal and dignified Joseph Nicholson Room, named after the second owner of the property, is furnished from Mr. Nicholson's inventory, a document unearthed during research. The Isaac Cannell Room is filled with game tables appropriate to the days when it was an integral part of the original tavern.

Bedrooms are decorated in several styles. Three are done in formal colonial: one with pencil post twin beds, one with a lace canopied double bed, and one with cannonball four-posters. All have wing chairs for reading, fresh colors, and beautiful hardwood floors. The T.W. Elliason Suite has

been restored to its Victorian origins. The bedroom and separate sitting room are decorated with high-back massive beds, a tufted settee, decorative friezes, and a busy floral carpet.

The White Swan's continental breakfast is special because it employs the talents of a gifted local baker and includes fresh-squeezed orange juice and grapefruit juice. Served in the Isaac Cannell Room, guests may request that breakfast be delivered to their door instead.

Chestertown, an important seaport in the early 1700s, is one of those special American towns that still reflects its moment of prosperity. The seat of Kent County and the home of Washington College, the town retains a great measure of grace and atmosphere.

WHITE SWAN TAVERN , 231 High St., Chestertown, MD 21620; (301) 778-2300; Mary Susan Maisel, hostess. Closed two weeks per year (usually early February). Six guest rooms in house, one attached "summer kitchen" suite, all private baths. Rates: $75 to $125, double occupancy; $25 per extra occupant; rates include light breakfast. Good dining nearby, especially in season. Children welcome; no pets; no credit cards. Area offers local museums, walking tours, recreation, wildlife preserves.

DIRECTIONS: from Chesapeake Bay Bridge (Rte. 50-301), take Rte. 301N to Rte. 213. Turn left on Rte. 213 to Chestertown, approx. 15 miles. Cross the Chester River Bridge and turn left at first stop light (Cross St.). Turn left again at next light (High St.). Inn is in middle of block on right.

Lovegrove's kitchen is the oldest and most rustic of the guest rooms.

THE ROSEBUD INN

Return to another time

When a body wearies of the daily grind and longs to escape to a simpler life, to a place where time seems to stand still, the village of Woodsboro awaits.

Once you arrive, the place to hang your hat is the Rosebud Inn, a solidly comfortable and immaculate guest house. The inn is owned by Alice and Albert Eaton, ex-city folk who fell in love with Woodsboro's bucolic charm and never turned back.

From the outside, the Rosebud is a solid, red brick, Colonial Revival home, with a wide, wraparound veranda supported by classical Ionic columns. The house was built in 1920 by Woodsboro's most prominent citizen, Dr. George F. Smith, founder of the Rosebud Perfume Company, which remains in operation next door to the inn, manufacturing rose-scented salve in sweet little tins. It is inside, however, where one truly appreciates the inn, for the physician spared no expense, installing marble and slate fireplaces, glistening oak floors inlaid with maple and walnut;

fine woodwork; oak paneling; and stained glass windows bearing the likeness of his beloved rose.

The Eatons have renovated and refurbished the house to a gleaming finish. Each guest bedroom is beautifully appointed, and the Eatons have added many small touches that make one feel thoroughly at home.

THE ROSEBUD INN, 4 North Main Street, Woodsboro, MD 21798; (301) 845-2221; Albert and Alice Eaton, hosts. Open all year. Six rooms and one cottage share 5 bathrooms. Rates: $80 to $85 double with continental breakfast. Children over 6 welcome; no pets; Visa/MasterCard accepted; German spoken. Tennis, swimming, boating, fishing, riding, antiquing nearby. Three country restaurants within walking distance.

DIRECTIONS: from I-70, I-270, or I-340 take U.S. 15 north 3 miles past Frederick to Rte. 26 East and turn right to Rte. 194. Left for 6 miles on 194 to Woodsboro and inn.

The Dining Room's woodwork and detailing is original to the house.

SPRING BANK INN

The rebirth of a stylish rural home

In 1880 gentleman farmer George Houck spared no expense when he built the most stylish home rural Frederick County had ever seen. Constructed of red brick, the house was given a Gothic Revival bay window, columned veranda, and gabled, fish-scale patterned slate roof. It was further embellished with elegant Italianate windows and an ornate belvedere for viewing the beautiful vistas of the surrounding countryside.

A century later the house captured the imaginations of Beverly and Ray Compton, who noticed it while on a bicycle tour of the area. Captivated as well by the rich history and architectural charms of Frederick, they soon bought Spring Bank Farm and embarked on a massive and much-needed restoration. Since the Comptons open bedrooms to overnight guests as each room is completed, today's guests are attending the birth of an inn and the rebirth of a house, with such fine details as frescoed ceilings, original brass hardware, louvered shutters, hand-marbled slate fireplaces, and hand-grained woodwork revealing themselves in the process.

Ray's family has been in the antiques business for several decades, and this expertise shows in many of Spring Bank's furnishings. High-ceilinged bedrooms easily accommodate full Victorian bedroom sets, canopied beds, and easy chairs. Plans are in the works to convert the third floor, which gives access to the belvedere, into an antiques shop.

SPRING BANK INN , 7945 Worman's Mill Rd., Frederick, MD 21701; (301) 694-0440; Beverly and Ray Compton, hosts. Elegant 1880 rural home that combines Greek Revival and Italiante architecture. Open year-round. Six guest rooms, one with private bath. Rates $60–75 single, $70–85 double. Hearty continental breakfast. No children under twelve; no pets; no smoking in home; Visa/MasterCard/Discovery/American Express/checks. Appalachian trail close by; trout fishing; historic district to explore. Wide range of good restaurants in town.

DIRECTIONS: from I-70, I-270, or 340, take U.S. 15 north about 5 miles, driving past Frederick. Look for "mile 16" marker; turn right at next road onto Rte. 355 south. Inn is ¼ mile south on left.

The common room, where guests meet for coffee.

RICHARD LIPPENHOLZ PHOTOGRAPH

THE SHIRLEY MADISON INN

A period-style hotel

A true in-town lodging, The Shirley Madison has period style without being prissy or pretentious, and is a comfortable place in which to experience turn-of-the-century living. The Park Court is a sister lodging which adjoins the main building across a common courtyard that is set up with tables during nice weather.

Charming stone carvings and marble pillars complement the red-brick façade of the 110-year-old main building. Inside, common rooms and a beautifully-papered parlor flank a winding oak staircase leading up to guest rooms. The rooms, all individually appointed, are furnished with an interesting assortment of Victorian and Edwardian antiques, and an equal measure of comfort. The small, vintage open-grille elevator offers an alternative to climbing the stairs.

A continental breakfast is presented buffet-style, and the hosts are friendly and helpful, often beyond duty—even an absent guest's dog may be taken out for a walk.

The inn is located in the historic Mount Vernon section, near Baltimore's elegant Washington Monument, and only minutes from the Walters Art Gallery.

THE SHIRLEY MADISON INN, 205 West Madison Street, Baltimore, MD 21201; (301) 728-6550; Stanley Gondzar, mgr., Irene Borowicz, ass. mgr. Open all year. 25 rooms with private baths, 12 with kitchenettes, 4 with parlors. Rates: $55 to $105 single; double $10 extra. Includes continental buffet breakfast, evening sherry, tea and coffee all day. Children welcome (under 12 free); small pets welcome; 3 smoking floors, 1 nonsmoking floor; Polish and French spoken; Visa/MasterCard/American Express/Diners Club. Parking on premises. Near Baltimore's North Charles St. restaurants, shops, and galleries.

DIRECTIONS: west of Washington monument off Charles St. north.

NATIONAL PIKE INN

The antiques capital

"We're here and available," says Terry Rimel. "We give our guests as much hospitality as they want." At the National Pike Inn you can play the parlor organ, have breakfast in bed, and feel like a part of the family.

Conveniently located between Baltimore and Frederick, New Market has been dubbed the "Antiques Capital of Maryland." More than thirty antiques stores lure the collector here to shops specializing in folk art, clocks, early lighting, porcelain, jewelry, and Victorian furniture.

The guest rooms in the inn are air conditioned and provide fresh flowers and fruit. The Victorian Room has a four poster covered with a rosebud and mint-green chintz spread, a green tapestry Victorian settee, a Cheval mirror, and carved cherry wood dresser. The Canopy Room has steps leading up to its canopied bed, a chenille spread, a piecrust table, and fireside bench.

NATIONAL PIKE INN, 9–11 Main Street, P.O. Box 299, New Market, MD 21774; (301) 865-5055; Tom and Terry Rimel, hosts. Open all year. Four guest rooms with private and shared baths (suite available). Rates: $60 to $100 includes full breakfast. Special weekly rates and on stays over two nights. Children over ten; no pets; smoking permitted; Visa/MasterCard.

DIRECTIONS: from I-70 take exit 62 to Rte. 75 and go north 1 block to Main St. Take left on Main St. (Rte. 144) for about 3 blocks to top of hill to inn in center of town.

The richness and warmth of the parlor.

SOCIETY HILL HOPKINS

Four periods to choose from

The first room you notice is the charming parlor with its floral couch and matching wallpaper border, faux-finish mantel, etched-glass Victorian chandelier, handsome artworks, and lace panel curtains. Guests often relax here with a cup of coffee or a glass of wine.

The twenty-six guest rooms in this Spanish revival building have been arranged into four different periods: Federal, Victorian, Art Deco, and Contemporary. Guests are invited to reserve that period room that suits their mood or sense of fantasy.

Gray, lavender, peach, and blue offset the patterned rugs in the Federal room. The wallpaper border is a classical Adams frieze, and the mahogany armoire, Chippendale-style chairs, draped valances, and old prints enhance the period effect.

The Victorian room features a dressing mirror, wicker desk, white iron sweetheart bedstead, marble-topped tables, and lace curtains, while the Art Deco room has black lacquer furniture, Chinese-style lamps, twenties prints, and touches of period maroons and greys.

Finally, the contemporary room in browns and persimmon, accented in green, has a bed with brass headboard, rattan night stands, a pine armoire, and Hitchcock-style chair.

The monotony of the usual assemblage of small hotel rooms will not be found here; appointments do not smack of the decorator's art. Instead the charm of European bed and breakfasts and the warm hospitality of American country inns combines in a uniquely exciting blend.

SOCIETY HILL HOPKINS, 3404 St. Paul Street, Baltimore, MD 21218; (301) 235-8600; Joanne Fritz, innkeeper. A historic building in an historic neighborhood. Open year-round. Twenty-six guest rooms, including suites, all with private baths; some with kitchenettes. Rates: $70–$135. Continental breakfast. Children welcome; no pets; smoking permitted; major credit cards accepted. Within walking distance of Baltimore Museum of Art, one block from Johns Hopkins University.

DIRECTIONS: call for directions.

SOCIETY HILL GOVERNMENT HOUSE

Baltimore's official bed and breakfast

These adjoining historic townhouses have been completely renovated and refurbished into Baltimore's premier bed and breakfast establishment. The project was the brainchild of the dynamic mayor, William Donald Schaefer. Painstakingly researched for historical accuracy, the complex was worked on for three years before it could offer hospitality in the style and manner for which Baltimore is noted. Swathed in Bradbury and Bradbury wallpaper, bedecked in Scalamandré and Schumacher fabrics, and outfitted with both antiques and fine reproductions, this grande dame has never appeared more glamorous.

Gifts from well-wishers are displayed everywhere: a silver-and-gilt chandelier from the Rouse Corporation, Louis Prang's oriental ceramic lithographs from the Walters Art Gallery, and a figurine from Mayor Ed Koch.

The décor of the guest rooms, clearly influenced by the Federal period, reflects a traditional Baltimore style. Sitting areas in guest rooms offer a table and desk and TV. Guests choose from one of two continental breakfasts brought to their room at a specified time.

In addition to providing hospitality to bed and breakfast guests, the house often hosts official government functions in the splendid library, reception hall, and dining room. His Honor, the mayor, maintains an elegant suite for accommodating dignitaries, such as the Mayor of Rotterdam.

Another function performed here is the training of small groups of unemployed area citizens as housekeepers, bartenders, hostesses, and waiters to satisfy Baltimore's burgeoning need for hospitality services.

Historically correct and graciously managed, the Society Hill Government House is a premier bed and breakfast serving Baltimore and the greater community—yet another jewel in Baltimore's crown.

SOCIETY HILL GOVERNMENT HOUSE, 1125-1129 N. Calvert Street, Baltimore, MD 21202; (301) 752-7722; Linda Cooley, innkeeper. Open year-round. Eighteen guest rooms, all with private bath and individual heating and cooling systems. Rates: $110–$130. Continental breakfast included. Children welcome; no pets; smoking permitted; major credit cards accepted.

DIRECTIONS: call for directions.

TWIN GATES B & B

Baltimore comfort

Twin Gates is only fifteen minutes north of Baltimore's exciting Inner Harbor, but it seems a world removed. The surrounding grounds are lush, expansive, and private. Gwen and Bob Vaughan decorated the house using a palette of soft blue, peach, cream, and beige. The first-floor common rooms, with fourteen-foot ceilings, feel spacious, and the inn's old-fashioned front porch, furnished with white wicker and bedecked with the flags of the U.S. and Maryland, provide an added dimension of charm and comfort. Each bedroom is furnished with every thoughtful amenity, from extra pillows and blankets to a home-baked "sweet dream" on pillows at night.

Gwen shines in the kitchen each morning, concocting such delectibles as strawberry short-cake or peach-and-orange-drenched French toast, known as "fuzzy navel." Early evening finds Bob in charge of the wine and cheese hour, during which guests recuperate from the rigors of the day and enjoy relaxed conversation.

TWIN GATES BED & BREAKFAST, 308 Morris Avenue, Lutherville, MD 21093; (800) 635-0370; Gwen and Bob Vaughan, hosts. Open all year. Seven rooms, 3 with private baths, 4 share 2 baths. Rates: $85 to $95, with lavish, full breakfast and bedside snack. Children over 12 welcome; no pets; no smoking; Visa/MasterCard/American Express; checks accepted. Flower gardens on premises. Tennis and cycling in area. Baltimore area famous for seafood restaurants.

DIRECTIONS: call for specific details, depending on which direction you are coming from.

Right, innkeeper Norma Grovermann in front of the lovely Georgian building she and her husband have made into a delightful bed and breakfast.

PRINCE GEORGE INN

The first Annapolis bed and breakfast

Capital of the state of Maryland, and once capital of the nation, Annapolis is a mecca for history buffs, preservationists, seafood lovers, and sailors. The United States Naval Academy, St. John's College, art galleries, historic mansions, and Chesapeake Bay are all within walking distance of the Prince George Inn.

Historically correct in its loving restoration, the inn has been pampered by Bill and Norma Grovermann, two preservationists who fought to establish the first of Annapolis's bed and breakfasts. Charmingly decked out in Victoriana and all manner of ephemera, there are eye-catching details that intrigue, such as the large carved mirror which hung in the White House during the McKinley administration when Norma's grandfather was a jeweler to the White House. The "so Victorian" parlor boasts persimmon sofas, tufted velvet side chairs, nautical paintings, vintage photos, lacework, and peacock feathers garnered from birds raised by Norma's daughter.

Each of the four guest rooms is uniquely memorable, and one, a Turkish room, has a sultry feeling highlighted by twin brass beds, tapestries, ferns, hanging fans, an armoire, and intricate panels rescued from a mosque.

A deluxe continental breakfast buffet is served in the sunny, glassed-in side porch, and includes tasty treats that Norma creates. After breakfast, it is worth exploring the tiny corner "antique shop" near the breakfast room, that catches the spill-over of the Grovermann's "things you'd like to take home."

A spacious private garden, with a gazebo, adds another dimension to this 1884 Victorian Italianate house. It is no surprise that it is letter perfect. After all, it is one of a dozen houses that the Grovermanns have rescued and restored.

PRINCE GEORGE INN, 232 Prince George Street, Annapolis, MD 21401 (301) 263-6418; Bill and Norma Grovermann, owners. Open all year. Four guest rooms, 2 with private baths and 2 sharing. Rates: $75 to $85 per room, including deluxe buffet breakfast. Children 12 or over welcome; no pets; no smoking in guest rooms; Visa/MasterCard. Situated in Annapolis Historic District with 20 restaurants within walking distance, Naval Academy 2 blocks, Capitol building 1 block.

DIRECTIONS: inn is 3 blocks from harbor in downtown Annapolis.

WASHINGTON, D.C.

KALORAMA GUEST HOUSE

A cosmopolitan clientele from around the world

Hidden away from the bustle of the city on a quiet residential street, the Kalorama Guest House is a home away from home. Its thirty-one well appointed rooms are put together with a cozy mix of fine antiques and grandmother's attic that includes beautiful Victorian bedsteads, armoires, and old Singer sewing machines that have been converted to tables.

PHOTOGRAPHS BY MICHAEL ACH

Wrought iron park benches serve as seating for breakfast in the brick-walled dining room.

Vintage photographs, old advertising prints, and portraits decorate the walls, and vases of fresh flowers lend fragrance and color to the public rooms. A generous continental breakfast is served in the brick-walled dining room where wrought iron park benches beside marble top tables afford guests from around the world the opportunity to meet and converse. Friendships can be furthered sipping afternoon sherry before a crackling fire.

Holidays are taken seriously here with a party at Halloween, stockings hung in guest rooms at Christmas, and baskets delivered to all at Easter. The fun-loving staff is attentive, friendly, and always ready to help with directions for sightseeing or museum going. Located in the Adams Morgan section, a vibrant neighborhood of old townhouses, antiques shops, and ethnic restaurants, the Kalorama is a five-minute taxi ride from downtown and all that Washington has to offer.

Noteworthy architectural details highlight a substantial old building.

Left, sherry is served in the gracious public rooms.

THE KALORAMA GUEST HOUSE at Kalorama Park, 1854 Mintwood Place, N.W., Washington, DC 20009; (202) 667-6369; Rick Fenstemaker, gen'l mgr., Tamara Wood, host. Open all year. Thirty-one rooms, some with private baths. Rates: $40 to $95, with full continental breakfast and afternoon sherry. There are no provisions for small children; no pets; checks, major credit cards accepted; smoking permitted. Limited parking space may be reserved in advance for $4 per night. Over 50 ethnic restaurants to choose from in a 2 block radius.

DIRECTIONS: from Baltimore south on I-95, take the beltway 495 west toward Silver Spring to exit 33. South on Connecticut Avenue towards Chevy Chase. Pass the zoo entrance in the 3000 block and count 4 stop lights and turn left on Calvert St. Go to 2nd stop light and turn right on Columbia; 2 blocks down turn right on Mintwood.

Co-owner/host Frances Randall.

DUPONT CIRCLE

International décor

There is something about this Dupont Circle location that has a European feeling. Maybe it is the neighborhood, filled with art galleries, foreign embassies, and private museums. Or the cafés and interesting architecture along the streets. Whatever the reason, this bed and breakfast fits right in, with an Australian hostess and sophisticated décor.

Built as a private home in 1895, this Victorian townhouse has high ceilings, large windows, and a sense of spaciousness that belies its urban location.

Innkeeper Frances Randall exudes warmth and graciousness amid the beautiful interior she's created. Multicolored carpets from the Far East cover the floors and an intricately carved 300 year-old Chinese opium bed serves as a sideboard/table in the parlor. There is an ever-growing collection of contemporary European paintings.

Three very large guest rooms offer queen-sized beds and private baths. The front room on the third floor has an especially nice feel, with a craftslike iron canopied bed positioned in the turret of the house. The interior of the turret rises up into a cathedral ceiling with skylights above the bed.

Breakfast is buffet style and gives guests an opportunity to appreciate Frances' culinary expertise. Formally trained as a gourmet chef in Europe, she will serve a special dinner or brunch, by arrangement, in a dining room filled with antiques.

The lodgings are close to many Washington attractions. And after a busy day out on the town, a great place to recoup is on the peaceful rooftop terrace of this inn.

DUPONT CIRCLE. A Victorian townhouse with 3 guest rooms, all with private baths, 1 with Jacuzzi. Frances Randall and Victoria Conway Wakefield, owner/hosts. Open all year. Rates: $100 per room, including buffet continental breakfast. Children over 6 welcome; socially acceptable pet welcome; smoking limited; all credit cards. Dinner parties and brunches served by arrangement. Variety of fine dining within walking distance. Directions given when making reservations. *Represented by B' n Breakfast Ltd. of Washington, D.C., (202) 328-3510.*

Superbly disciplined elegance.

Some of the art nouveau collection.

LOGAN CIRCLE

Extravagantly restored

Extensively restored by two loving owners, this one-hundred-year-old Victorian mansion features original wood paneling, stained-glass niches, ornate chandeliers, and a Victorian-style lattice porch and gardens. A mecca for lovers of "Art Nouveau," its walls are covered with highly selective and artfully framed posters, prints, magazine covers, and advertising art. The hostess, a tireless collector, is constantly adding new pieces to her collection.

In addition to the house's own beautiful appointments, the owners have incorporated some Victorian gems rescued by architectural salvagers: gilded mirrors, intricately carved mantels, and glistening English tiles. Floral patterns combine with silks, violet walls, wainscoting, draperies, oriental rugs, Eastlake furniture, and vintage floors, creating a romantic ambiance. One of two parlors houses a working player piano with silk-fringed turquoise shawl.

Each of the five guest rooms is singular and charming. An additional ground floor apartment offers complete privacy and comfort. Guest room furnishings include antique quilts, wicker, greenery, shutters, wash bowls, a Jacobean desk, and a four-poster bed.

Overlooking a fountain and rose arbor, the latticed porch seduces with a promise to banish worldly cares. Here one can effortlessly return to the romance and elegance of by-gone days.

LOGAN CIRCLE. Century-old Victorian mansion with gardens, terrace, and Victorian-style lattice porch. Open year-round. Five guest rooms, with shared baths; apartment with private bath. Rates: $60-$70 single, $70-$80 double, apartment $75 single, $85 double. Continental breakfast included. Children welcome; no pets; smoking permitted; MasterCard/Visa/American Express. Logan Circle is an area in transition; guests are advised to drive rather than walk at night. *Represented by Bed 'n Breakfast Ltd. of Washington, D.C.*

Owner/host Ed Perlman.

MOUNT PLEASANT

Every room a treat

Urbane, artistic, and splendidly restored are a few of the words that might describe this bed and breakfast. The house itself is a turn-of-the-century Edwardian townhouse, but what really makes your stay here so special is the multi-talented and affable innkeeper, Ed Perlman.

Ed has been an English teacher, an art gallery owner, a real estate developer, and a nationally recognized interior designer, with work featured in *Architectural Digest*. His accomplishments are re-

Relax and read a good book.

flected in his bed and breakfast, which is filled with wonderful antiques, sculpture, rich colors, and special attention to all the details that make life enjoyable. Linens are crisp and white, bathrooms are piled with thick fluffy towels, each room has terry robes and every morning you're greeted by rich aromatic coffee that Ed blends and grinds himself.

Add to all that a few more of Ed's talents: topiary plants throughout the house, headboards he designed himself, and unique woven trims on curtains and bedskirts, from his collection of antique textiles. Another collection, early nineteenth century blue and white platters, serves up Ed's freshly baked family recipe biscuits or stuffed bread pastries.

The house is in the colorful Adams Morgan neighborhood, an extremely popular and fashionable area filled with ethnic and unusual restaurants, shops, nightclubs, and art galleries. Adjacent are the National Zoo and Rock Creek National Park.

MOUNT PLEASANT. An Edwardian townhouse with 5 guest rooms, including a suite, with king, queen, and twin beds. Some have private baths and some share. Ed Perlman, owner/host. Open all year. Rates: $65 to $95, per room, including sit-down continental-plus breakfast. Children over 12 welcome; no pets; smoking outside only; Spanish and German spoken; all credit cards. Garage parking on premises by reservation. Excellent dining nearby. Directions given when making reservations. *Represented by B 'n Breakfast Ltd. of Washington, D.C., (202) 328-3510.*

BED & BREAKFAST RESERVATION AGENCIES

The concept of Bed and Breakfast in the United States is rapidly expanding. To facilitate this phenomenon, reservation agencies are quickly cropping up, resulting in rapidly changing information. Many of the agencies listed below have been in existence for some time; others have been organized recently. Do not be surprised if there are changes when you contact them.

Connecticut

BED AND BREAKFAST, LTD., P.O. Box 216, New Haven, CT 06513; (203) 469-3260; Jack Argenio. Write, sending SASE, or call between 5–9 P.M. weekdays and any time weekends. Period homes, estates, farms. *125 listings statewide.*

COVERED BRIDGE BED & BREAKFAST, P.O. Box 447A, Norfolk, CT 06058; (203) 542-5944; Diane Tremblay. *Northwest Connecticut, southern Berkshires, Hudson Valley, and Connecticut shoreline, Southern Vermont.*

NUTMEG BED AND BREAKFAST AGENCY, P.O. Box 1117, West Hartford, CT 06107; (203) 236-6698; Michelle Souza. 9:30 A.M. to 5 P.M. Monday through Friday. Vacation homes, restored historic homes, relocation. *Connecticut.*

District of Columbia

THE BED & BREAKFAST LEAGUE/SWEET DREAMS & TOAST, P.O. Box 9490, Washington, DC 20016; (202) 363-7767; Millie Groobey. *Washington, D.C., and adjacent suburbs.*

BED 'N' BREAKFAST LTD. OF WASHINGTON, D.C., P.O. Box 12011, Washington, DC 20005; (202) 328-3510; Jackie Reed 10–5 weekdays, 10–1 Saturday. *Washington metropolitan areas, specializing in the historic districts.*

Maine

BED & BREAKFAST DOWN EAST LTD., Macomber Mill Road, Box 547, Eastbrook, ME 04634; (207) 565-3517; Sally Godfrey. Private homes at lakeside, countryside, town, or coast. *Maine.*

BED & BREAKFAST OF MAINE, 32 Colonial Village, Falmouth, ME 04105; (207) 781-4528; Peg Tierney. Weekdays 6–11 P.M.; weekends 10 A.M. to 10 P.M. *Coastal, islands and mountains in Maine.*

Maryland

AMANDA'S BED & BREAKFAST RESERVATION SERVICE, 1428 Park Avenue, Baltimore, MD 21217; (301) 225-0001; Betsy Grater. 9:00 A.M. to 5:00 P.M. weekdays. Private homes, yachts and small inns. *Baltimore, Maryland, and nearby states.*

THE TRAVELLER IN MARYLAND, P.O. Box 2277, Annapolis, MD 21404; (301) 269-6232; Greg Page. 9 A.M. to 5 P.M. Monday to Thursday; 9 A.M. to noon Friday. Yachts, inns, private homes. *Maryland, London, Paris.*

Massachusetts

BED AND BREAKFAST ASSOCIATES, Bay Colony, Ltd., P.O. Box 166, Babson Park Branch, Boston, MA 02157; (617) 449-5302; Arline Kardasis. *Eastern Massachusetts.*

A BED & BREAKFAST ABOVE THE REST, Box 732, Boston, MA 02146; (800) 677-2262, (617) 277-2292; Colleen Hartford. 10 A.M. to 4 P.M. Victorian townhouses and Beacon Hill homes. *Boston/Brookline, Cambridge, Cape Cod, Nantucket, Plymouth, Gloucester.*

BED AND BREAKFAST CAMBRIDGE AND GREATER BOSTON, P.O. Box 665, Cambridge, MA 02140; (617) 576-1492; Pamela Carruthers. 9 A.M. to 6 P.M. Monday–Friday; 10 A.M. to 3 P.M. Saturday. Private and vacation homes of every description. *Boston, Cambridge, and Lexington.*

BED AND BREAKFAST CAPE COD, Box 341, West Hyannisport, MA 02672; (508) 775-2772; Clark Diehl. Country inns, sea captains' houses, host homes. *Cape Cod, Martha's Vineyard, Nantucket, Gloucester, and Cape Ann.*

BERKSHIRE BED AND BREAKFAST HOMES, P.O. Box 211, Williamsburg, MA 01096; (413) 268-7244; Eleanor Hebert. *Private homes in western Mass. from Sturbridge to the Berkshires; southern Vermont, eastern New York state, District of Columbia.*

HOST HOMES OF BOSTON, P.O. Box 117, Waban Branch, Boston, MA 02168; (617) 244-1308; Marcia Whittington. 9 A.M. to 12 noon, 2 to 4:30 P.M. *Covers Boston and select city suburbs.*

PINEAPPLE HOSPITALITY, INC., P.O. Box F821, New Bedford, MA 02742; (508) 990-1696; Robert Mooz. 9 A.M. to 5 P.M. weekdays. Homes or small inns. *Six-state area of New England.*

New Hampshire

NEW HAMPSHIRE BED & BREAKFAST, P.O. Box 146, Main Street, Ashfield, MA 01330; (413) 628-4033; Ernie Taddei. Country classics, waterfront, mountain views, farms. *New Hampshire.*

New Jersey

BED & BREAKFAST OF NEW JERSEY, INC., Suite 132, 103 Godwin Avenue, Midland Park, NJ 07432; (800) 992-2632; Aster Mould. Vacation homes, refurbished mansions, apartments. *New Jersey, including seashore, and Delaware River area, northeast Pennsylvania, and New York. Package tours.*

New York

ABODE BED & BREAKFAST, LTD., P.O. Box 20022, New York, NY 10028; (212) 472-2000; Shelli Leifer. *Manhattan and Park Slope.*

ALTERNATE LODGINGS INC., P.O. Box 1782, East Hampton, L.I., NY 11937; (516) 324-9449; Francine and Robert Hauxwell. *The Hamptons from Westhampton to Montauk Point.*

THE AMERICAN COUNTRY COLLECTION, 984 Gloucester Place, Schenectady, NY 12309; (518) 370-4948; Beverly Walsh. *Northeastern New York, Vermont, Western Massachusetts.*

A REASONABLE ALTERNATIVE, INC., 117 Spring Street, Port Jefferson, NY 11777; (516) 928-4034; Kathleen Dexter. *Long Island along the North and South shores of Nassau and Suffolk Counties.*

BED AND BREAKFAST (& BOOKS), 35 West 92nd Street, New York, NY 10025; (212) 865-8740; Judith Goldberg. A unique service offering a selection of hosts who work as photographers, psychologists, lawyers, dancers, teachers, and artists, with special knowledge of New York's rich cultural life. *New York City.*

BED & BREAKFAST U.S.A., P.O. Box 418, South Egremont, MA 01258; (800) 255-7213; Carol Jones and John Black. *New York City, New York State, New England, Florida, and Caribbean.*

CITY LIGHTS BED & BREAKFAST LTD., P.O. Box 20355, Cherokee Station, New York, NY 10028; (212) 737-7049, Fax (212) 535-2755; Dee Staff and Yedida Nielson. 9:00 A.M. to 5:00 P.M. Monday to Friday; 9:00 A.M. to 12:00 P.M. Saturday. Hosted and unhosted apartments from studios to four bedrooms in apartment houses and brownstones. Two night minimum stay. *Manhattan, Park Slope, Brooklyn Heights, and Queens. Ask about Europe.*

NEW WORLD BED AND BREAKFAST, 150 Fifth Avenue, Suite 711, New York, NY 10011; (800) 443-3800; (212) 675-5600; Kathleen Kruger. 9:30 A.M. to 5 P.M. Monday to Friday. Hosted and unhosted apartments in high rises, brownstones, and carriage houses. Two night minimum stay. *Manhattan.*

NORTH COUNTRY BED & BREAKFAST RESERVATION SERVICE, Box 286, Lake Placid, NY 12946; (518) 523-9474; Lyn Witte. 11 A.M. to 8 P.M. daily. Private homes, country inns, and mountain resorts. *The Adirondack Mountains from Glens Falls north to the Canadian border, and from Lake Champlain west to Watertown.*

RAINBOW HOSPITALITY BED AND BREAKFAST, 466 Amherst St., Buffalo, NY 14207; (716) 283-4794; Georgia Brannan. *Rochester, Niagara Falls, and Buffalo areas and 8 counties of western New York.*

URBAN VENTURES, INC., P.O. Box 426, New York, NY 10024; (212) 594-5650; Mary McAulay. *Manhattan and other boroughs.*

Pennsylvania

ALLABOUT TOWN—B&B IN PHILADELPHIA, P.O. Box 567, Valley Forge, PA 19481-0562; (800) 344-0123, (215) 783-7838, Fax (215) 783-7783; Carolyn J. Williams. Town, country, historic and ski locations, city and country inns. *Philadelphia, Brandywine Valley, Valley Forge.*

BED & BREAKFAST CENTER CITY, 1804 Pine Street, Philadelphia, PA 19103; (215) 735-1137; Karen and Gordon Andresen. *Philadelphia's Center City, Rittenhouse Square, Antique Row, Society Hill, University City, Art Museum area.*

HERSHEY BED & BREAKFAST RESERVATION SERVICE, P.O. Box 208, Hershey, PA 17033; (717) 533-2928; Renee Deutel. Call from 10 A.M. to 3 P.M. *Lebanon and Hershey, Lancaster, Gettysburg, Harrisburg.*

BED & BREAKFAST OF PHILADELPHIA, P.O. Box 1252, Gradyville, PA 19039; (215) 358-4747 (800) 733-4747. Joan Ralston. *Philadelphia, its suburbs, and surrounding historic countryside, including Valley Forge, Chadds Ford, New Hope, and Amish countryside.*

BED & BREAKFAST OF SOUTHEAST PENNSYLVANIA, 146 W. Philadelphia Ave., Boyertown, PA 19512; (215) 367-4688; Patricia Fedor. Old farmhouses, town and suburban houses. *Reading and Allentown area, Bethlehem, and Lancaster county.*

REST & REPAST BED & BREAKFAST SERVICE, P.O. Box 126, Pine Grove Mills, PA 16868; (814) 238-1484; Linda Feltman and Brent Peters. 8:30 A.M. to 11:30 A.M. weekdays, and 6:30 P.M. to 9:30 P.M. Closed Thursday and Sunday. Farms, National Historic Register homes, apartments. *Main Penn State campus vicinity plus Huntington and Altoona areas.*

Rhode Island

BED & BREAKFAST REGISTRY AT NEWPORT, 44 Everett Street, Newport, RI 02840; (401) 846-0362; Norma Johnson. 9 A.M. to 7 P.M. weekdays, Sat. 1 to 5 P.M. April to Oct. Restored colonials, Victorian mini-mansions, and homes by the sea. *Newport.*

HISTORIC NEWPORT INN ASSOCIATION, P.O. Box 981, Newport, RI 02840; (401) 846-7666. *12 Newport inns.*

Vermont

VERMONT BED & BREAKFAST, Box 139, Browns Trace, Jericho, VT 05465; (802) 899-2354; Sue and Dave Eaton. *Vermont only.*